Laura Ingalls Wilder

Laura
Ingalls
Wilder

Tanya Lee Stone

DK PUBLISHING

LONDON, NEW YORK, MUNICH,
MELBOURNE, AND DELHI

Editor : Beth Landis Hester
Publishing Director : Beth Sutinis
Designer : Mark Johnson Davies
Art Director : Dirk Kaufman
Production Controller : Jen Lockwood
DTP Coordinator : Kathy Farias
Photo Research : Anne Burns Images
Cartographer : Ed Merritt

First American Edition, 2009

14 15 16 17 10 9 8 7 6 5 4 3
003-DD519-Feb/2009
Published in the United States
by DK Publishing
345 Hudson Street
New York, New York 10014

DK books are available at special discounts
when purchased in bulk for sales promotions,
premiums, fund-raising, or educational use.
For details, contact:

DK Publishing Special Markets
345 Hudson Street
New York, New York 10014
SpecialSales@dk.com

A catalog record for this book is available
from the Library of Congress.

ISBN 978-0-7566-4508-3 (Paperback)
ISBN 978-0-7566-4507-6 (Hardcover)

Printed and bound in China
by South China Printing Co., Ltd.

Discover more at
www.dk.com

Contents

Introduction

Beloved Author

Laura Ingalls Wilder introduced generations of children to the essence and spirit of America's pioneer days. She came from a family of pioneers, moving many times during her youth and braving new experiences in the wide-open spaces of unsettled America in the 1860s, 70s, and 80s. As a grown woman, she told her daughter Rose the stories of her childhood, and she later offered them to the world in her Little House books for young readers. Millions of fans have fallen in love with Laura's stories, and for a long time, many thought of her books as a purely autobiographical account of her life.

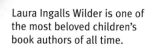

Laura Ingalls Wilder is one of the most beloved children's book authors of all time.

But in truth, although Little House books are based on her life, there are many differences between the details of Laura's life and the stories her books tell.

It is easy to see how this could be confusing. Laura, the main character of the Little House stories, is very similar to the real Laura. But some details in her books (and the long-running television series *Little House on the Prairie,* which strayed even further from the truth) do not match the life she lived. In order to paint a vivid picture of what pioneer life was like and impart ideas to her readers, Wilder chose to fictionalize some things. She stayed true to fact whenever possible.

It is interesting to read the initial draft of Laura's autobiography, called "Pioneer Girl," which was never published. Many of her books for children stemmed from this careful work of memoir—although it stops in 1889, after she had been married for four years. Studying "Pioneer Girl" makes it a bit easier to spot the differences between the real and the fictional Laura.

From the moment the first Little House book was published in 1932, Laura Ingalls Wilder was an important and permanent fixture in children's literature. Today, her books are as popular as ever, and she has given us a lasting, literary legacy. And Laura Ingalls Wilder's true biography is every bit as exciting as her stories. For fans of of her books, students of history, and young readers everywhere, it is a story well worth telling.

chapter 1
From the Big Woods to the Prairie

Laura Ingalls Wilder came from a family of adventurers. Her parents were pioneers, and so were all of her grandparents. Charles Philip Ingalls, Laura's father, was born in the southwestern part of New York State in 1836. He was one of Lansford and Laura Ingalls's 10 children. When he was nine years old, Charles and his family moved from New York to Illinois and settled in a prairie town about 40 miles (64 km) west of Chicago. But by the time Charles was 17 years old, the open landscape was striped with more

Covered wagons such as these were used by pioneers to travel long distances with their belongings.

and more fences, and Lansford grew restless. The family packed up to move again—this time to Jefferson County, Wisconsin.

Charles was a lot like his father. He loved the prairie. He loved the high grasses and the open spaces. He also inherited Lansford's tendency to grow restless when places grew too crowded.

In Wisconsin, where the Ingalls family was moving, there lived a girl named Caroline Lake Quiner. Her parents, like Charles's, had also moved from the eastern part of the country (Connecticut, in her case) to the Midwest, stopping in Ohio and Indiana before migrating to Wisconsin. Henry and Charlotte Quiner had seven children. Caroline was the fifth, born in 1839. Her father died when she was just a little girl, and things were very hard on the family. But by the time Caroline was nine her mother was able to buy some land, and the family moved to a farm just a few miles away from what would later become the Ingallses' farm.

Caroline's mother, Charlotte, had once been a schoolteacher, and education was very important to her. She made sure her children learned to read and write when they could find time between chores. She made sure they found time to play, too. They waded in the river and romped in the woods.

When Caroline was 10, her mother married a man named Frederick Holbrook, who became a kind stepfather

Caroline Quiner and Charles Ingalls were married in February 1860.

to Caroline and her siblings. About five years later, their new neighbors arrived. It is easy to imagine how these two families—the Quiners and the Ingallses—both good neighbors with several teenage children close in age, became friendly. Charles Ingalls and Henry Quiner—Caroline's brother—were fast friends, opening the door for their siblings to meet . . . and to court. Henry Quiner married Polly Ingalls—Charles's sister—in February 1859. The following year, in February 1860, the smart and steady Caroline Quiner married lively Charles Ingalls with his bright blue eyes and love of fiddle playing. And a year after that, Charles's brother Peter Ingalls married Caroline's sister Eliza Ann Quiner.

Despite all of this happiness among the families, however, hard times fell on Charles's father, Lansford, and he lost his land. True pioneer that he was, Lansford decided to leave Jefferson County and start over farther west. The Ingalls clan—with seven children still remaining under the care of their parents—was on the move again. But the traveling party in covered wagons was going to be even

> *"Neighbors took turns helping each other to construct their cabins before winter set in."*

—Gertrude Yanish, a relative of the Ingallses

larger this time: All three married pairs of Quiner-Ingalls children went west along with Lansford.

The group settled near Pepin, Wisconsin, in what would come to be called the "Big Woods" in books written by the yet unborn Laura Ingalls Wilder.

In September 1863, Charles Ingalls and Henry Quiner—still close friends and of like minds—bought land together from a man named Charles Nunn. The brothers-in-law agreed each to live and work on his own half of the land, and they helped each other well. They built a cabin for each couple, planted gardens, caught fish, hunted wild game, and cared for their cows. Caroline and Polly did their part, too, with everyone working from sunrise to sunset to provide the food and supplies their families needed. This was typical of the lives of pioneers. They also made sure there was time to enjoy each other's company. Caroline and Charles both loved to tell stories, and Charles liked to sing and dance and play his fiddle.

Charles Ingalls's fiddle is on display at the Laura Ingalls Wilder Home and Museum in Mansfield, Missouri.

> *"Who would wish to leave home and wander forth in the world to meet its tempests and storms?"*
>
> —Caroline Quiner, written when she was a little girl

Henry and Polly Quiner soon had three children. And then, on January 10, 1865, Charles and Caroline Ingalls had their first child as well: a daughter named Mary Amelia. She and her father shared the same birthday, a fact that delighted the family. Two years later, the couple welcomed another daughter. Laura Elizabeth Ingalls was born on February 7, 1867. She was named after her great-grandmother, Laura Colby Ingalls.

Caroline was content in the Big Woods, and although Laura was probably too young to form clear memories of her own, she later wrote about the cozy feeling in the cabin, with her mother singing and her father sitting by the fire, looking lovingly at his family.

As the area became more populated, however, Charles's wanderlust stirred. He was not unhappy, but something was missing for him. He longed once again for the open spaces of the prairie, which he remembered from his childhood. There was a feeling in those prairies that he could not get in the woods where they lived.

In the spring of 1868, Charles and Henry sold their land to a Swedish settler named Gustaf Gustafson. Then

they loaded up the two covered wagons with everything they owned—Charles and his family in one, Henry and his family in the other—and left the Big Woods of Wisconsin.

Until they found a new place to settle and build their homes, the wagons would serve them well. Day after day they rode, through Minnesota, then Iowa, then Missouri. Some days were dismal—no other people in sight, stormy weather, deep rivers to cross. Other days were joyous. At night they would stop to cook dinner over a fire, make camp, then wake to tackle another day's adventure.

Their intended destination was Chariton County, Missouri, where Charles and Henry had purchased some land. It is not completely clear whether the two families ever arrived there. At some point along the way, Henry and Polly

This is a reproduction of the house near Pepin, Wisconsin, where Laura was born.

decided to go back to the Big Woods of Wisconsin, retracing their path back home. But Charles was still in search of an ideal spot. He, Caroline, Mary, and Laura journeyed farther west, into Kansas.

The flat, treeless land and big open sky in Kansas were just what Charles had been looking for. And the new town of Independence, Kansas, must have held some appeal for Caroline. Even though there was only one store, and other buildings were just starting to be built, there were people to meet, and neighbors to greet. But town life was not what Charles had in mind. He had come to homestead, to develop a farm for his family. So their horses, Pet and Patty, pulled the wagon farther on, with the family's bulldog, Jack, trotting

Homesteaders would stock up on supplies at depots like this one, carrying things back to their homes in ox-driven carts.

along behind. Finally, Charles settled on a spot about 13 miles (21 km) west of Independence. It was September 1869.

This was the place. There was a strong creek that ran through the land, providing a good supply of water. And the trees that lined the banks of the creek would provide enough timber to build a house. All in all, the area seemed just about perfect.

Charles had gotten some advice in Independence about where to find a good parcel of land for homesteading, but the land he arrived at was actually on the Osage Indian Reserve. It was not public land at all, and it is not known for certain whether Charles was aware of this. There were certainly other settlers nearby, as well as a census taker who recorded their family and noted Charles as a "carpenter" in the 1870 census report.

The Homestead Act of 1862

On May 20, 1862, President Abraham Lincoln signed the Homestead Act. The intention was to encourage migration and farmland development outside the 13 original American states. The homesteading process had three steps: file an application for 160 acres of public land, improve the land by building a dwelling and growing crops for five years, and apply for the deed to the land. The homesteader would then become the legal owner of the property. In general, a person was eligible as long as he was either a U.S. citizen or planned to become one.

Perhaps Charles and the other settlers thought that the Indians would soon be driven west, as other tribes had been, with so many white settlers encroaching on their lands. Or perhaps Charles was too preoccupied with plowing the soil and getting a house built to stop and file the homesteading paperwork that would have revealed that he was on the land illegally. In any case, he began to build, and the settlers and the Osage co-existed without too many troubles during the Ingalls family's early days in the area.

This 19th century painting of Osage people highlights their colorful beads and jewelry.

Day after day, Charles looked for trees that were straight enough to use, cut them into logs, and hauled them to the spot where the cabin would be built. In "Pioneer Girl," Laura recorded some of her memories from this time. She remembered that her father (or "Pa," as she called him), took a trip to a nearby town and brought back "a cook stove, a window to put in the window hole and some lumber to make a door."

Laura and her sister Mary played in the high grasses, and in the mud by the creek. Laura loved to be outside, following deer tracks or watching the birds and rabbits. In the evenings, Pa played his fiddle and sang.

That summer, the whole family came down with terrible fevers and was quite sick. So were many of the other settlers in the area. We now know that the illness was spread by mosquitoes, which were a pesky problem in the prairie lands every summer. A doctor who lived in the area treated the family, and they were soon well again.

Then one day Pa took Mary and Laura on a walk that led them straight into the Osage camp. The Osage had left on a long hunting trip, so Pa knew it was safe to bring his girls there. Laura and Mary spotted small flashes of color on the ground.

This is an example of an Osage camp. The Osage tribe was eventually driven out of the area where the Ingalls family had settled.

They made a game out of gathering up the red and green and blue beads that had been left behind.

When it was time to go home, they walked back to the cabin. And there they found a new addition to their family! On August 3, 1870, Caroline, or "Ma," gave birth to a third daughter. A neighbor, Mrs. Scott, had come to help Caroline with the delivery. Laura's new baby sister was named Caroline Celestia. The family called her Carrie.

When Laura's family had first arrived in the area, they had occasional visits from the Osage. The Indians seemed to want only food, or simply to show their presence on the land that was rightfully theirs. A show of hospitality and a few pieces of corn bread from Laura's mother appeased them.

One of the Ingallses' neighbors, Eliza Wyckoff, also experienced a visit from the Osage: "They stayed about half an hour, and laughed and talked to each other. . . . They called on each family in the neighborhood. They were on dress parade."

But that was all changing—and in a way, this wasn't surprising. After all, the Osage were being pushed off the lands they had been allotted by the government. The settlers were disturbing their hunting grounds. Their trails were being trampled. And in some cases, the damage settlers did to the Osage community was intentional. The Indians were growing angry. In "Pioneer Girl," Laura remembered hearing their drumming and war chants from the cabin. To her, they "sounded much worse than the wolves."

American Indians

When the first colonists arrived in North America in the 1600s, Indians already lived there. By the 1800s, the new Americans were still claiming Indians lands as their own. In some cases, tribes were simply pushed off their land. In others, tribal leaders signed treaties with the government, agreeing to move away. There was frequent contact between pioneers and Indians. Sometimes it was friendly; sometimes it was not.

Troubled times were ahead. The situation with the Osage people was heating up. Eliza Wyckoff recalled a second Osage visit to her cabin much different from the first: "An Indian came and showed Uncle and Aunt and I how they would come and shoot through the cracks and scalp us and tear down our houses."

The government offered the Osage a new treaty that doubled the price it had originally offered to pay for their lands. In return, the Osage would have to leave and find new land in Indian Territory (present-day Oklahoma). The Osage eventually accepted.

That fall the Osage moved on, in long lines, on horseback. They would never return—they had been pushed from their lands forever. Laura and her family watched the departing Indians pass by their little house on the prairie.

chapter **2**

The Big Woods Beckons

Tensions calmed when the Osage left the prairie where the Ingalls family lived, but something else soon came up that may have spurred their next move. Pa got a letter from Gustaf Gustafson, the man who had agreed to buy their old home near Pepin, Wisconsin. Gustafson could not get enough money together to make good on their agreement, and asked Charles to come and take the land back.

Charles and Caroline decided that would be the best thing to do, although it must have been difficult to walk away from the results of their

A pioneer family poses with a covered wagon, similar to the kind the Ingallses used. The fabric sides allowed riders fresh air in good weather and protection from the elements.

hard work. Charles was probably happy to pack up their lives again—as always, he loved the excitement of the journey. Laura was just four years old when she and her family left Kansas

"[We traveled] for days and days, sleeping in the wagon at night, until we were very tired."

–Laura

to make the long trip back east in the spring of 1871. She was big enough now to sit on the bed at the back of the wagon and look out over the backboard to see what they left in their tracks. They traveled "for days and days, sleeping in the wagon at night, until we were very tired."

The journey stretched on and on, and the Ingalls family rarely saw other people. The wagons they did see were usually going west, the direction most pioneers headed in search of unsettled lands. From time to time big storms rolled in, and the family would huddle together for warmth—and also to stay away from the rain-soaked canvas sides of the wagon. Once, the Ingalls had to cross a stream so deep that the wagon floated part of the way. When they had traveled as far as Missouri, the family found an empty house where they could stay for a little while, while Pa worked to earn some money. Then they would continue the journey to Wisconsin.

Laura's indoor pastimes included needlepoint. This sampler (her first) shows the kinds of stitches she was learning.

When it was time to move on, Pa decided that their horses, Pet and Patty, were too tired and small to make the rest of the long trip. The wagon was just too heavy for them to pull any farther. So he traded them for bigger horses. He also included the family's pet bulldog, Jack, in the trade, "because Jack wanted to stay with Pet and Patty as he always did."

When they arrived in Wisconsin, there was a big family welcome. Grandpa and Grandma Ingalls were there, and Uncle Henry and Aunt Polly too. Since Gustaf Gustafson had not yet moved out of Pa's house, Pa, Ma, and the girls moved in with Uncle Henry's family for a few weeks. Henry and Polly had four children—Louisa, Charley, Albert, and Lottie. Lottie and Laura were about the same age, and Laura later remembered having had wonderful times playing with her cousins before Ma and Pa moved their family back into their own house.

When Ma sent six-year-old Mary to join her cousins at the Barry Corner School down the road, Laura was a little envious. She was still too young for school, and her baby sister Carrie was too young to be much fun to play with. Pa was usually out clearing land or hunting, Ma was busy with housework—and Laura may have felt bored. She helped Ma as much as she could, of course, but she was happier when she could walk down the road a bit and meet Mary on her way home from school. The sisters would play or walk through the woods, which still seemed new and exciting. They had been used to wide, open prairies; here there were forests to explore.

At night, Ma would read to the children, and Pa would tell stories and play his fiddle. Both Ma and Pa sang songs that filled Laura's heart with laughter. Pa was playful, and often called Laura his "little half pint of cider half drank up." One of her favorite games was "mad dog." During a game of mad dog, Pa would "put his fingers through his hair to make it stand on end" and then chase Mary and Laura around on all fours.

Laura was thrilled when her parents allowed her to go to school in October. However, she only attended for a few months, until Christmas. Her parents may have reconsidered, deciding it would be better if she waited until she was a little older after all. Or perhaps the deep snow drifts kept the younger ones home in winter.

Countryside Dangers

We often think of life in the cities as being more dangerous than life in the country, but rural areas have their dangers, too. This was especially true in pioneer times, when there were great stretches of land with few people, and often no lawmen around. In the area near where Laura lived, there were instances of violent crime documented. As picture-perfect as these times may seem in storybooks, safety certainly must have been on the minds of parents as they sent their children on the long walks to school or to a neighbor's house.

Pa was able to trade furs in exchange for other supplies his family needed.

No matter the season, Laura was an energetic girl who loved the outdoors, where she could run and climb fences or trees. She learned to wash, iron, and sew, but the chores she preferred were more active—such as going out to the woodpile to gather the wood chips that would help start the fire in the stove. Laura thought her sister Mary was much more ladylike than she was. When she was a grown woman (but still long before she had published her first book) she was interviewed by her local newspaper, the *Missouri Ruralist,* about her childhood. "I was a regular little tomboy," she told the reporter.

The farm provided many things for the family. Pa had planted wheat and corn, and they also had a garden for vegetables as well as a cow for milk. But there were some things the family needed that couldn't be produced on the farm. So Pa trapped animals and collected their furs, which he could trade for supplies in town. Then he would set off for Pepin with his furs, returning several days later with much-needed goods and supplies such as sugar, fabric, salt, and kerosene.

Before long, Pa began to grow restless again. He had an "itchy foot." He longed to live in open prairies instead of the Wisconsin woodlands, where stubborn tree sprouts kept trying to grow back in his cleared fields, and wild game was growing scarcer as the area became more populated. The covered wagons he saw heading west added to his restlessness. He wanted to move again.

Ma, on the other hand, liked the wooded landscape, and having good neighbors nearby. She did not yearn for unsettled spaces the way her husband did. But she went along with his wishes, and they made the decision to leave the Big Woods.

Trading posts allowed pioneers to trade for supplies they couldn't farm or make on their own. Families could buy flour, sugar, cloth, and even tin cans for storing preserved food.

chapter **3**

Prairie Plight

I t was late fall in 1873 when Pa and Ma decided to leave the Big Woods. Just as Laura's Uncle Henry had agreed to go west with Pa the first time they left Wisconsin, this time Pa's brother, Uncle Peter, and his family would go with them for part of the journey. Both families were headed for Minnesota, but Peter planned to stop in the southeastern part of the state, while Pa hoped to settle in the southwest. Pa sold his farm for the second time, and the Ingallses loaded up their belongings.

Everything the Ingallses needed to start a new home went on the wagon—dishes, pots and pans, bedding, clothing, and any small pieces of furniture that wouldn't weigh them down.

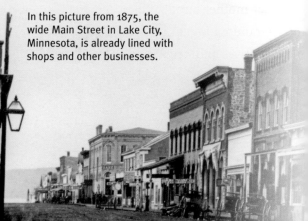

In this picture from 1875, the wide Main Street in Lake City, Minnesota, is already lined with shops and other businesses.

Pa's fiddle, too, was packed safely amongst the quilts, and his gun was hooked near the seat of the wagon for protection. No one knew for certain what dangers they might encounter along the way, so Pa wanted to be prepared.

SCARLET FEVER

Scarlet fever is caused by a bacterial infection. Symptoms include high fever, sore throat, and a red rash all over the body.

For a while, they all stayed at Uncle Peter's, making plans. While they were there, the children became ill with scarlet fever. "We were all going west in the spring," Laura later wrote, "and this sickness worried the fathers and mothers for we must drive across the lake before the ice got soft." Indeed, the snow had been falling, and Pa and Uncle Peter did want to be sure they crossed Lake Pepin before the ice began to thaw—but the parents were probably more concerned about their children's health. Thankfully, everyone got better soon, although Laura still needed to be kept out of the cold. At the beginning of February 1874, her mother bundled her up in the wagon, Grandpa and Grandma Ingalls waved good-bye along with other relatives and neighbors, and the two families were on their way. They crossed the lake safely, and arrived in Lake City, Minnesota.

Lake City was much larger than Pepin, and it had a library, railroad, and hotels. The Ingallses stayed in one of the hotels for a few days, and they celebrated Laura's seventh birthday while they were there. Her father gave her a "pretty little book of verse" called *The Floweret*.

Then the families started on their way again. Before long, they came upon an empty cabin by the side of a creek. Laura wrote that the cabin was "so close to the creek that if we had fallen out of the back window we would have dropped into the water." The grown-ups decided that the weather was still too cold for them to travel very far in the wagons, so they all settled into the house until warmer weather set in. Laura was still not herself after suffering from scarlet fever. She wrote: "My ears hurt me so much I couldn't play."

Still, things were cozy and peaceful in the cabin by the creek. A fire burned in the stove, and warm quilts were piled on the beds. In "Pioneer Girl," Laura wrote: "One night Mary lay sleeping beside me but I lay awake looking through the bedroom door at the firelight flickering and the shadows moving in the room outside. Pa was sitting in the shadows where I couldn't see him but I could hear his fiddle singing. It was all so beautiful it made my throat ache."

The route the Ingalls family traveled covered hundreds of miles.

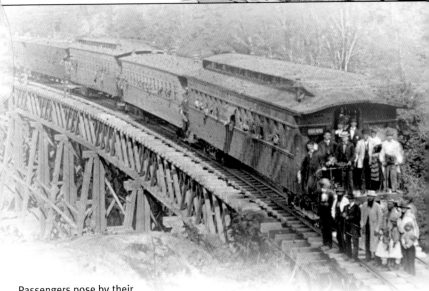

Passengers pose by their
train on a journey through
Minnesota, around 1890.

When springtime arrrived, the
covered wagons rumbled on once more. But soon it was time
to part ways. Uncle Peter and Aunt Eliza headed to a farm near
the Zumbro River in southeastern Minnesota, and Laura's
family continued on.

Their journey would be relatively smooth. Laura wrote:
"The grass along the road was fresh and green in the
springtime and it was a delight to camp at night in a little
nook somewhere beside the way. . . . We'd see the sun go
down, hear the birds twitter their sleepy good nights. . . .
Sometimes Pa would sit awhile by the campfire and play
his violin." Pa would hunt small animals for dinner, and the
family would picnic in the grass.

One evening, Laura heard an odd sound in the distance.
It seemed like it was calling to her. When she asked Pa what

it was, he told her it was a train whistle. She looked out and saw a train speeding past on tracks that were only about a year old. It was heading to a stop near Walnut Station, Minnesota—soon named Walnut Grove.

The Ingalls family was now in Redwood County. They had traveled about 200 miles (322 km). The area had just the kind of terrain Pa was looking for: dark, rich soil, rolling prairie, and not many trees to clear for farmland. He chose a site less than two miles (3 km) from the new, small town of Walnut Grove. For a while, the Ingallses lived in a dugout house on the property, built right into the banks of Plum Creek. (Today, all that remains of the dugout is an impression in the ground, but the site is maintained and marked with a sign so people can visit it.)

They joined the new Congregational church, and the family became friends with the other settlers, who came from as far away as

Dugout Houses

Dugout houses were common on the prairie, usually serving as temporary shelters while people earned enough money (or found the time) to build a frame house. They were built into a hillside or the bank of a creek or river. They generally had a dirt floor, a ceiling made of hay, and one exposed wall with a door and a window. Dugouts stayed warm in the winter and cool in the summer, so they were a good choice for the climate of the prairie.

Norway, Ireland, England, and Sweden. They were especially fond of a family

Walnut Grove, Minnesota, pictured here about 20 years after the Ingallses moved there, was a small but orderly town.

called the Nelsons. Laura wrote: "I was with her [Mrs. Nelson] so much that Pa said I talked English like a Swede and I could easily understand when Mrs. Nelson talked her language with the other Swede neighbors." (They were actually Norwegian.)

The first winter brought blizzards, and there was a lot of time spent indoors, but Ma always had a book at the ready to help pass the time. By the spring of 1875, Pa had readied the fields for planting wheat. He had also built a proper house, and the Ingalls family soon moved out of the dugout and into their new home. It was a two-story house with glass windows and a new cook stove.

There was also a new schoolhouse in Walnut Grove for Laura and Mary to attend. The girls would pull up their skirts and wade across Plum Creek, then walk along the dusty wagon road to get there.

Laura made some good friends in Walnut Grove. Her best friend was Nettie Kennedy, who was eight years old, like

Pioneers like Pa often used oxen to pull the plow.

Laura. But as in most communities, there were also people who did not get along well. The person Laura had the most trouble with in Walnut Grove was a girl at school named Nellie Owens.

Nellie was two years younger than Laura, and the daughter of the man who owned Walnut Grove's general store. Nellie was a snob and treated Laura and Mary as though they were inferior because they were "country girls" and she lived in the town. Laura later based the character of Nellie Oleson in her novels on her former classmate.

At home, Laura helped with the chores. She took the cows to pasture, washed the dishes, and helped her mother look after four-year-old Carrie. The family was busy and happy, and their spirits were high as they waited to harvest their first crop of wheat.

Then, just as everything seemed perfect, a sunny day turned cloudy. But the clouds were not rain clouds. Instead, swarms of grasshoppers appeared overhead, millions upon millions of them. They rained down from the sky—and onto the wheat fields. All the family's hard work was ruined as the grasshoppers devoured the crops. The grasshopper infestation ruined Pa's fields and many others across the prairie. Farmers lost crops (and the income those crops would have brought), schools and businesses closed, and some whole towns became deserted. Many pioneers gave up and left the prairie for good.

Pa kept his usual upbeat spirit, but he had to leave home to find work. Laura recalled: "Pa told us good-bye, put on his hat and carrying his coat over his shoulder, started walking east to find work in the harvest fields." In Pa's absence, Mr. Nelson looked out for the family. It was particularly hard on Ma to have Charles gone, as she was pregnant with their fourth child.

Finally, in the fall of 1875, Pa returned.

People tried to save their fields by catching as many grasshoppers as they could during the infestation.

chapter 4
City Life

In October, the family moved into town for the winter, to a house "behind the church and not far from the schoolhouse." This made it easier for the girls to get to school through the bad weather. It also put Ma closer to the things she would need when a new baby was born. "Coming home from school one day, we found . . . a little brother beside Ma in the bed." Charles Frederick Ingalls arrived on November 1, 1875. The family called him Freddie.

That winter was a mild one, and the Ingalls family didn't stay in town for long. "While the snow and ice were still on the ground and on the creek," Pa moved the family back to the farm. But Ma suddenly became very ill, and was in desperate need of a

The Ingallses moved into the town of Walnut Grove in the winter of 1875.

doctor. Laura started to go to the Nelsons for help, but the creek waters had risen and were about to swallow up the little bridge behind the house. She remembered: "It terrified me, for the footbridge was standing away out in the middle of the stream, with yellow, foaming water running on both sides and just over the top of it." Luckily, Mr. Nelson saw her and motioned for her to turn back, so she hollered out her message, and

Pa and Ma Ingalls pose for a formal portrait, with Ma wearing the hair comb Laura and Mary bought for her.

Mr. Nelson got word to the doctor. Ma improved not long after that.

One day, before setting out on the walk home across the prairie from school, Laura and Mary stopped at a store in town. They saw a beautiful hair comb they knew their mother would like, but they didn't have the 50 cents to pay for it. The store owner offered to hold it for them, and the sisters saved the pennies they earned from doing extra chores until they had enough to buy it as a surprise for Ma. Times were hard, and there was little money for anything that wasn't a necessity, so their gift was extra special.

The Great Grasshopper Infestation

The grasshoppers that wreaked havoc in 1875 had been terrible, but the land had started to recover a year later. Unfortunately, there was still the problem of the eggs that had been laid. Laura wrote: "The ground looked like a honeycomb it was so full of the little round holes where the grasshoppers had laid their eggs." When the eggs hatched in summer 1876, the prairie was devastated once again. Throughout Dakota Territory and Minnesota, farms and businesses were ruined by the marching, munching army of grasshoppers. Many pioneers lost everything they had.

Soon, the prairie was green again, and Pa was hopeful that the new wheat crop would be plentiful. After the grasshopper infestation the year before, they needed a good crop more than ever. But soon the grasshopper eggs that had been laid the previous year began to hatch, and all was lost. Once again farms were devastated. There was no wheat, which meant no money and no food.

Many people left the prairie in search of new opportunities. Pa discussed the situation with Ma, and with their neighbors. Their friends, William and Mary Steadman, planned to leave for Burr Oak, Iowa, where they had bought a hotel. They asked Pa if he wanted to help run it. This was likely not Pa's favorite kind of work, but he thought it was for the best.

In July 1876, Pa sold his land, and the covered wagon was packed to the brim once again. On the way to Burr Oak, the family stopped to visit Uncle Peter and Aunt Eliza in eastern Minnesota—thankfully, the grasshoppers had not reached that far east. All was well for a time, with the cousins happily reunited and enjoying the summertime. Laura was nine, as was one of her favorite cousins, Peter. They romped and played, and helped with the chores.

Then one day, Ma and Freddie became very sick. A doctor came a few times and Ma recovered, but Freddie did not. Laura wrote: "Little Brother got worse instead of better and one awful day he straightened out his little body and was dead." It was August 27, 1876, and Freddie was only nine months old. The family was grief-stricken. It broke their hearts to leave him behind, but little Freddie was buried near Uncle Peter's place. They had to move on to Burr Oak without him.

Burr Oak, Iowa, had once been on a major wagon route, and had plenty of houses and stores, and even a church. But the new

The Burr Oak hotel was home to the Ingalls family when they first moved to Iowa.

railroads did not go through Burr Oak, and the town was becoming a bit run down now that it was no longer on a major travel route. Laura wrote: "It was not a new, clean little town like Walnut Grove. It was an old, old town and always seemed to me dark and dirty."

For the first few months the family lived at the hotel, but it was crowded and noisy, and very different from what they were used to. Ma and Pa were worried about exposing their girls to the influence of some of the lodgers. "Pa and Ma didn't like the saloon next door either and we were a little afraid of the men who were always hanging around its door." To make matters worse, the Steadman and Ingalls families were not getting along.

Laura was 10 now, and seems to have been aware that money was tight in their family. She later wrote, in a letter to her daughter: "Steadman handled the money and someway beat Pa out of his share. I don't suppose there was much."

Soon the family moved out of the hotel and into an apartment above the grocery store down the street, and Pa went into business with a mill owner. But they were still living too close to the saloon. When Ma became pregnant again, Pa was even more eager to find a safer place for his wife and daughters. In January 1877, he rented a small brick house on the edge of town, next to a pasture and some woods.

Pa took on some additional odd jobs, one of which may have been tending other people's cows. The family now had room to have a cow of their own again, too. Laura loved the walk she regularly took to help take the cows to pasture and back. In "Pioneer Girl," she wrote: "Even if it rained, the wet was nice on my feet and the rain felt good on my face and on my body through my thin, summer clothes."

Laura was doing well at school and improving her math skills, an accomplishment of which she was very proud. And she and Mary liked their reading teacher, Mr. Reed, very much. Laura later wrote: "I have always been grateful to him for the training I was given in reading." She and her sister would read aloud at night when they still lived above the grocery, and Laura recalled "Pa knew, but did not tell us until later, that a crowd used to gather in the store beneath to hear us read."

On May 23, 1877, a daughter was born: Grace Pearl Ingalls. Little Grace was a healthy baby with bright blue eyes and blonde hair. The family was happy . . . but their situation was still precarious. Once again, big changes were just around the corner for the Ingalls family.

Grace Ingalls was born on May 23, 1877. Laura wrote of her: "Her hair was golden like Mary's and her eyes were blue and bright like Pa's."

chapter 5

Welcome Back to Walnut Grove

In Burr Oak, life was pleasant and happy for Laura. She loved "the rippling brook and wondered at the beauty of the world, while I wriggled my bare toes down into the soft grass." She got to go to school, read, play, and spend time outdoors. She and her sister Mary were enjoying themselves.

Unfortunately, their parents did not seem as happy. The Ingallses had come to Burr Oak to recover from the hard times in Walnut Grove, but Pa had only found temporary jobs. With so many mouths to feed and money scarce, it was difficult to refuse any kind of work. A woman who lived nearby even offered to pay for Laura to

Around 1880, tough, fun-loving Laura (standing) was about 14 years old. Carrie (left) and Mary (in a dress matching Laura's) were the more "ladylike" Ingalls sisters.

go live at her house and help out. Laura breathed a sigh of relief when she heard her mother politely turn the woman down! But Ma and Pa

> *"It seemed that we wanted nothing so much as we wanted to keep going west!"*
>
> —Laura

knew one thing for sure: Burr Oak wasn't the place for them. It was time to move on.

In 1878, the family left Burr Oak and traveled back to Walnut Grove. The sad songs Pa had been playing on his fiddle turned cheerful once again. It may seem strange that after everything that had happened, the family decided to head back west. Laura herself remarked: "Everything came at us out of the West. . . . Storms, blizzards, grasshoppers, burning hot winds and fires . . . yet it seemed that we wanted nothing so much as we wanted to keep going west!" And now, at almost 11 years old, Laura was moving once again.

When the Ingallses arrived once again in Walnut Grove, they moved in with their old friends John and Cedelia Ensign. Pa got a job in a store and another working for Will Masters, who owned the Masters Hotel. The Ingallses shared living expenses with the Ensigns, and all the children got along well. Laura was happy to be back with some of her other friends, too, especially Nettie Kennedy.

Of course, Nellie Owens was still there, as well. And now there was Genny Masters, whose uppity attitude was as bad as

Laura liked to play outdoors like the boys in this 1873 drawing of games by a rural schoolhouse.

Nellie's. Laura had become an excellent judge of character, and was a natural leader. When she decided to ignore Nellie and Genny, who both tried to be the "boss" of the kids at school, they began to compete to win her favor instead!

Laura liked being in school, and loved the Friday-night spelling bees the best. And as always, she adored being outside. Although Mary did not approve and often told on her to Ma, Laura still preferred playing catch and racing around like the boys to acting the "proper lady" like Mary. Laura was proud of her ability to keep up with the boys. "Only one boy in school could throw faster than me, and not always could he do it," she later wrote.

Meanwhile, Pa worked hard to provide for his family. When Mr. Masters couldn't give him enough work, he took on different jobs to make ends meet, including doing carpentry and opening a butcher's shop. Pa was well liked and well respected in town. He was elected a trustee of the church, and became the town's first justice of the peace. When he had made enough money to build a house, the family moved again—this time, just down the road.

Laura was a hard worker, too, and did her part for the family. "Pa could not get much work and we needed more money to live on," she wrote. So when Laura was 11, she got her first job: working at the Masters hotel, for 50 cents a week. She set tables, washed dishes, and even cooked some of the meals. In the spring of 1879, when she was 12, Laura took a job caring for the ailing Nancy Masters (Laura called her "Nannie"). But Laura was homesick at Nannie's place, and it was scary work. Laura wrote: "I never knew at what moment Nannie would fall without a word or a sign and lie as if dead."

While the Ingallses were working hard to make a good life, they also enjoyed plenty of happy times. Pa taught the girls how to dance, and Ma loved being at home with her family, cozy and content. But that winter, Mary suddenly became very sick. She had a horrible pain in her head and a high fever. Laura later remembered: "One morning when I looked at her I saw one side of her face drawn out of shape. Ma said Mary had had a stroke." Although Mary got better, her eyesight suffered. The nerves in her eyes had been permanently

STROKE

A stroke occurs when blood flow to part of the brain is blocked, injuring the brain.

damaged, and she was going blind. "The last thing Mary ever saw was the bright blue of Grace's eyes," Laura wrote. Mary was not one to complain, and Laura learned patience from her sister. She became Mary's eyes, describing everything she could so her sister would not feel as much in the dark.

In the meantime, Pa was still scraping to get by, and still dreaming of open spaces. One day, his sister Ladocia (nicknamed "Docia") stopped to visit on her way to Dakota Territory, where she planned to live. Docia's husband, Hiram Forbes, worked for the Chicago and Northwestern Railway, which was building railroad tracks westward into Dakota Territory. Forbes needed someone to keep the books and run the company store. Pa was offered the job. The pay was 50 dollars a month—much more than he could make in Walnut Grove. Plus, there were homesteads nearby. Pa was excited for the new opportunity.

A crew of railroad workers lay tracks in 1887, opening new territories to travel and trade.

Ma, on the other hand, had had enough of moving! But she agreed to move to Dakota Territory if Pa would promise her that this would be the last move. While Ma and the girls stayed in Walnut Grove for the summer, Pa went on ahead to get started. Laura knew now more than ever how important it was to do her part for her family. She helped Ma look after the younger girls, and continued to help care for Mary.

When it was time to go, the Ingalls girls and Ma made the first part of the journey by train. This was their first train ride, and it took them to Tracy, Minnesota, where the rails stopped. (Past that point, workers were still laying down the tracks.) Pa met his family there with the wagon. All the while, Laura continued to act as Mary's eyes, painting pictures with her words so her sister could experience everything she did.

The Great Dakota Boom

Historians regard the year 1878 as the beginning of the "Great Dakota Boom." For the next eight years, Dakota Territory experienced enormous growth. The new railroads expanding into the Territory made it possible for people to get the supplies they needed—such as food, fuel, and building materials—and also gave farmers access to marketplaces. In sharp contrast to the slower arrival of settlers by wagon, the railroads brought people in by the tens of thousands. Towns sprang up around railroad stops, and farms were claimed nearby. Dakota Territory was so large it entered the Union in 1889 as two states: North Dakota and South Dakota.

Pa pulled the wagon into the railroad camp where he had been

Although not drawn to scale, this picture of the inside of a railway car gives a sense of how people traveled on trains at the time.

working all summer. Docia's daughter, Lena, was at the camp, too. Lena and Laura hadn't seen each other for a number of years, but they were close in age. Laura was happy to see her cousin and to have someone to play with. Lena even taught Laura how to ride a horse, an event Laura later used as the basis for a dramatic episode in her book *By the Shores of Silver Lake*.

As the workers made progress building the tracks, their job site (the end of the tracks) moved farther west. So the railroad camp, too, had to move westward, this time to Silver Lake—near present-day De Smet, South Dakota. Laura described the Silver Lake area as a "great, new country, clean and fresh around us." More family members were already at the new camp: Laura's Uncle Henry and her cousins Charley and Louisa. Henry was working on the railroad to earn money to go farther west.

Laura's family moved into one of the small shelters at the Silver Lake camp. The shelter was very basic, with straw mattresses for sleeping. But there was a lot to see outside. Laura walked Mary around and described the well-named silvery lake, the prairie grasses, and the layout of the camp. (Ma and Pa warned the girls to steer clear of the men working on the railroad.)

The Railroad

Today, we think of trains as ways to move people from place to place. But in the late 1800s, they were just as crucial for moving essential equipment and food to new settlements. As railroads extended west, so did access to the supplies that allowed towns to grow. Two railroad companies were largely responsible for the development of the Dakota Territory. The Chicago and Northwestern (C&NW) and the Chicago, Milwaukee, and St. Paul (the Milwaukee).

The one proper house belonged to the surveyor in charge.

SURVEYOR

The railroad surveyor was the engineer responsible for mapping and measuring where new tracks would be laid.

When the camp closed for the winter, Pa made an arrangement with the surveyor: Pa would watch over the camp with all its equipment and supplies and his family would live in

Silver Lake was beautiful and unspoiled territory when the Ingalls family lived there.

the warm, well-stocked surveyor's house for the season.

Laura loved the quiet of the area with the workers gone. Although the ground floor of the surveyor's house was only 12 by 15 feet (3.7 by 4.6 m), it was big by 1870s standards. Laura wrote: "There was one large room, kitchen, dining room and living room in one. From one side of this opened the pantry, a bedroom and the stair door between." The family snuggled into this house, dancing, listening to Pa's fiddle, playing checkers, and reading.

Meanwhile, Pa spotted a place near Silver Lake where he wanted to homestead. He knew that the new town of De Smet was to be built later that year—and that other homesteaders would soon crowd into the area. He did not want to miss his chance. Pa filed his claim in February 1880, soon after Laura's thirteenth birthday. That spring did bring a rush of settlers, just as Pa had predicted, and the

surveyor's house turned into a bustling boarding house offering food and shelter to travelers. Having already worked in hotels, Laura was well prepared to cook and clean for the boarders.

The surveyor's house where Laura lived is the oldest house in De Smet.

One of the lodgers was Reverend Edward Alden, a minister the Ingalls family had known in Walnut Grove. He had been "sent out into the west to plant churches along the line of the new railroad." Reverend Alden led a church service while he was staying with the Ingallses. He also told Ma and Pa about something that would later be of interest to Mary: a college for the blind in Iowa.

The surveyor's house has been restored to look like it did when Laura lived there. This room served as both the kitchen and dining room.

chapter **6**

On to De Smet

Putting his carpentry skills to quick use, Pa helped construct some of the first buildings in De Smet. One of them was a hastily built store on a lot Pa had bought in town. In April 1880, the Ingalls family moved into it. When an unexpected early blizzard struck, the snow blew right inside. "Pa was standing barefoot in it . . . he shook the snow off his socks and out of his shoes and put them on."

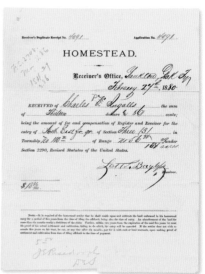

Pa filed this homestead claim early to beat the rush of oncoming settlers.

By this time, homesteaders were flooding through the area. "Slowly at first one a day, then later in crowds they came, wagon loads, hack loads, buggy loads of men stopped on their way to the forts and towns further west." Many stayed, and De Smet grew fast. There was a grocery store, a furniture shop, a saloon, a drugstore, a hardware store, a schoolhouse, and a few hotels. The wide open spaces were being replaced by a bustling town.

Laura preferred the quiet of the country to the noise of town, and she was glad when Pa decided it was time to move to their homestead claim.

There was a shanty there that Pa had quickly put up in order to keep away claim jumpers—people who tried to take over claims that had not yet been occupied. Laura would later recall: "The farm was home to us. Town was just a place to spend the winter."

The family worked hard to get their shanty in good shape. Pa worked on the walls, dug a well for water, and built a stable for the cow. The girls helped Ma clean and unload the wagon, making the little house homey.

The town of De Smet grew quickly in the 1880s. In this picture, horse-drawn buggies stand beside posts holding electrical wires.

> *"Snow drifts in one night were piled as high as the second stories of the houses."*
>
> —Laura

There were all kinds of jobs to do outside, too. Pa started a vegetable garden and planted small cottonwood trees near the house. Laura also helped make hay out of the prairie grasses, to be used as feed for the cow and horses. It was hard work for a young girl—pitching the grasses onto the wagon to dry and then piling the rough sticks into stacks—but she did it well.

The fall brought terrible blizzards, one after the other. The shanty was not going to protect the family through such bad weather, so they moved back into Pa's store in town. Unlike Laura, Ma preferred being around people—and there were now plenty of people in De Smet. (In the time that had passed, the population had grown to about 100.) But Laura thrived just the same. She was 13 now, and more aware of boys. On the way to school one day, one boy in particular caught her attention. Edward "Cap" Garland was a nice, outgoing young man. Laura later wrote that he was "tall and quick and he moved as beautifully as a cat. His yellow hair was sun-bleached almost white and his eyes were blue." Even though she caught the ball he threw her way that day, she soon tried to be less of a tomboy and a bit more ladylike.

Due to the storms, school was soon closed for the season. The blizzards continued through the winter. People tied ropes between their houses and stables in order to find their way home after feeding the cows and horses. It was dangerous to be outside for any length of time during a bad storm. The Ingalls family stayed huddled close to the fire, reading and telling stories. Pa tried to lighten the mood with his fiddle playing. And when the winds weren't whipping up, the children had fun playing in the snow.

The trains, which carried crucial supplies as well as people, started having trouble getting through to De Smet as early as November. The

Weather and Supplies

Pioneer towns depended on trains for food and fuel—and those trains depended on clear tracks to make it to the towns. Deep snow could be a disaster, stopping trains from traveling. Today, most everything we need is available nearby, but pioneers cut off from supply trains for the winter were in desperate situations. Only hard work and the will to survive kept people going through extended periods of bad weather.

last one to make it arrived in early January 1881. By that time, food and fuel were already running low throughout the town. The grocery store had nothing left to sell. People had to make do with whatever they had managed to save that would keep through the winter—mostly foods such as potatoes or preserves. Another girl who lived in De

The Wilders posed for this portrait around 1870, about 10 years before they befriended the Ingalls family. Almanzo is standing in the back. His brother Royal is seated, far left.

Smet that year, Neva Whaley Harding, remembered the effects of the blizzards: "Dad would walk to town once in a while and pick up what food he could find. . . . provisions were carefully parceled out so every family got a share, maybe only five pounds of flour."

Although it was hard on the hands, hay had to be twisted tightly into sticks to burn in the stove. Wheat was ground up in the coffee grinder to make flour for biscuits. "It seemed as though we had been grinding wheat and twisting hay for years," Laura wrote. And Neva recalled: "Hay does not hold heat very long so the house got mighty cold at night while we lay shivering and shuddering as we listened to the weird howling of coyotes."

Things were getting dire. The town of De Smet had no more wheat. But it was rumored that one nearby homesteader might have a good supply of it. Cap Garland and another young man from town, Almanzo Wilder, decided to brave the storm and make a deal with the homesteader before people began to starve. They bought up all the sacks of wheat the settler had to sell, and brought them back to the storekeeper who had given them the funds to pay for it. But when they found out the storekeeper wanted to charge the townspeople too much for the wheat, they got upset. Pa joined Garland and Wilder in insisting that the wheat be sold to their hungry neighbors for a fair price.

Imagine the relief when spring came and the snows began to melt! On May 10, a train finally made it through to De Smet. Laura recalled: "All the men in town were down at the tracks to meet it. . . . Our days of grinding wheat in coffee mills were over."

De Smet continued to grow and develop after the Ingallses had left. But later generations would still feel the snap of the cold Dakota winters.

chapter **7**

Bessie and Manly

Once again, Laura was thrilled to be able to leave town and go back to the house on the prairie. The spring of 1881 had brought a new onslaught of settlers, and the town was having another growth spurt. "I didn't much care for all these people," she wrote. "I loved the prairie and the wild things that lived on it, much better."

Laura had kept her promise to be Mary's eyes, and had helped her sister's education by reciting her own lessons out loud for Mary to hear. But Mary, a bright girl, wanted more out of school. When Laura was offered a job that summer at Clayson's dry goods store, she took it to help her parents pay for Mary to go to the school for the blind Reverend Alden had told them about. Laura missed Mary terribly after she left for Iowa in the fall, but knew it was the best thing for her sister.

This photo of Mary Ingalls was taken when she was a student at a school for the blind.

Laura was stronger and more independent than ever. As she attended school in town, she was again drawn to Cap Garland's smile and sense of humor. In November, after a prayer meeting at the new church in town, Almanzo Wilder asked if he could walk Laura home. Although she accepted, she wrote, "to be perfectly truthful, I was noticing Cap." Almanzo was almost 10

Laura drew this map later in life, based on her memories of De Smet.

years older than Laura, but he was a respectable young man with a homestead of his own, and Pa liked him. He walked her home several more times after that.

Meanwhile, a settler named Louis Bouchie arrived in town. He was hoping to find a teacher for his new school, located in a settlement 12 miles (19 km) away. Laura was

a strong student, but she was not yet 16, the required age for a teaching certificate.

The Ingalls house in the town of De Smet, South Dakota, was closer to the neighbors than Pa would have liked.

Laura earned her teaching certificate at a young age.

Nevertheless, she was offered the job—and at 20 dollars a month, it was difficult to turn down.

Laura may have been nervous about moving so far from her family for the school term, but she agreed to go. The superintendent of schools gave Laura a teacher's exam on December 10, 1883, and she passed. She was now officially a teacher.

Just a week later, Pa took Laura to the Bouchie School. Laura was a natural teacher and enjoyed herself while she was teaching, but living with the Bouchies was another matter all together. Mrs. Bouchie seemed miserable and made Laura feel the same. By the end of the first week, Laura was desperate to get out of the house. Happily, Almanzo arrived in his horse-drawn sleigh to drive her home for the weekend. This became a habit, with Almanzo driving Laura from De Smet to the Bouchie house each Sunday, and picking her up each Friday to go home.

Almanzo Wilder was a young man when he began to take an interest in Laura.

This picture of Laura was taken when she was 17. She was almost 10 years younger than Almanzo.

Pioneer Teachers

By the 1870s, it was common for both boys and girls to go to school into their high-school years. It may seem strange that many of the pioneer teachers were close in age to some of the students they were teaching. Some teachers were trained for their duties, and even traveled from the East to the settlements to find teaching jobs. But in other cases, the need for teachers was so great they simply had to pass an examination and demonstrate their scholarship. Many still needed to continue their own studies during the school term. And only single women were allowed to be teachers. Once Laura married, she could no longer teach.

On these long trips across the cold prairie, Laura and Almanzo got to know each other well. They even discussed what nicknames they should use for one another. Almanzo had a sister named Laura, so decided to call his friend "Bessie" as a nickname for Laura's middle name, Elizabeth. When Almanzo told Laura his brother Roy called him "Mannie," she thought he said "Manly"—and that suited her fine. And Manly didn't mind at all! Still, Laura said she did not have romantic feelings for him: "I was only going with him for the sake of being home over Sunday and fully

Almanzo gave Laura this book as a gift when they were courting.

intended to stop as soon as my school was out."

When the winter school term ended, she was very happy to go back to De Smet to stay. She also made it clear to Manly that they were simply friends. But he didn't let that bother him. He simply showed up while their other friends were racing around the snow in their sleighs and offered her a ride. Without thinking, Laura hopped in—and soon realized that perhaps she did feel something for Manly. This became even more apparent during her next job, which took her away from home again for a few months.

When Laura returned to De Smet in the fall, she and Manly spent a lot of time in each other's company. "I hadn't known that I missed him, but it was good to see him again, gave me a homelike feeling," she wrote. They took many carriage rides to break in his horses, and Manly often let her take the reins.

While he was courting Bessie, Manly also tended his homestead. In the spring of 1884, Laura took another teaching job nearby and worked for a dressmaker in town. She had changed a lot from the tomboy who didn't like to sew. Now she was quite accomplished at it, and had an interest in fashion that would last her a lifetime.

That summer, Mary came home from college for a visit. The whole family was back together again. Something else happened that summer, too. One night, after a carriage ride across the prairie, Manly asked Laura to marry him. She remembered: "He kissed me goodnight and I went into the house not quite sure if I were engaged to Manly or to the starlight and the prairie." In November, Manly left on a long trip with his brother Roy, not to return until the spring. But a week before Christmas, Manly came back. He hadn't been able to stay away from his fiancée.

Laura and Manly were married on August 25, 1885. She wore a black cashmere dress and insisted the word *obey* be removed from their wedding vows. The two entered into an equal partnership from the start.

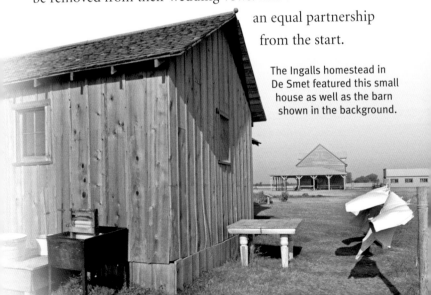

The Ingalls homestead in De Smet featured this small house as well as the barn shown in the background.

chapter **8**

Hard Times

The day before they were married, Manly took Laura's things out to his homestead shanty about two miles (3 km) to the north. The night of their wedding, everyone wished them well, and they drove home together as husband and wife. Laura Ingalls was now Laura Ingalls Wilder. It was the beginning of a new chapter in her life.

In addition to the property where the Wilders spent their wedding night, Manly had a second homestead lot that was a "tree claim," on which a settler had to promise to plant 10 acres of young trees. Manly had already satisfied the government's requirements for the first lot, so he built a lovely frame house with three nice-sized rooms

Laura and Manly wear their warm coats in this photograph, taken the winter after they were married.

on the tree claim. They even had carpet in the bedroom. There was a stable for the horses, and Laura's father had given them a cow.

For a short time, life was sunny. The couple ordered a set of dishes from the Montgomery & Ward catalog, complete with a creamer and sugar bowl, as well as a pitcher and several goblets. They rode the horses, did the chores, laughed, and visited friends. They planned to be equal partners in the business of wheat farming.

In the spring, Laura became pregnant. She hadn't necessarily wanted the life of a farmer's wife, but she loved Manly, so that was that. And she was capable of all sorts of tasks. She later said: "I learned to do all kinds of farm work with machinery. I have ridden the binder, driving six horses." Besides, Manly had been raised for this job, so he was a good partner to have. He had grown up on a large, successful farm in New York State. His parents had the means to run it and had taught him well, in addition to providing him with a good education. Unfortunately, there were unforeseen troubles ahead for the Wilders.

In 1886, a hailstorm ruined their first wheat crop. With the baby coming, the crops destroyed, and bills to pay, they needed to rethink their plans.

In the end, a mortgage on the first homestead lot gave them the money they needed. But they would have to live on that part of

MORTGAGE

A mortgage is an arrangement with a bank to borrow money against the value of a house or land.

In a drought, the soil may become so dry it cracks. The plants dry out as they lose their source of nourishment.

Manly's land, as they had when they were first married. They moved out of the little gray frame house and back into the shanty. Rose Wilder was born there on December 5, 1886. She was a large, healthy baby, blonde and blue-eyed.

Laura and Manly had high hopes for the next season, but they were unlucky again. Although they had a wheat crop, a drought had made it smaller. Then, not long after they harvested the grain, the barn where it was stored burned down, and it all went up in smoke. But Manly was determined. They wouldn't be giving up anytime soon. Sadly, tragedy struck again in the winter of 1888, when Laura and Manly both came down with diphtheria and became deathly ill.

Rose went to live with Laura's parents, who had given up homesteading for good and moved into town. She was only about two years old, but Rose later recalled: "Nobody knew what would become of my father and mother. . . . They had diff-theer-eeah; a hard word

DIPHTHERIA

Diphtheria is an extremely contagious, potentially deadly infectious disease that can make it difficult to breathe.

and dreadful. I did not know what it was exactly, only that it was big and black and it meant that I might never see my father and mother again."

Laura's little sister Grace kept a diary of that time, and wrote of Rose: "She is the best girl I ever saw. She can now say a good many words such as gramma and grampa and bread and butter and cracker." This record of their toddler daughter is the one ray of sunshine peeking out from all the darkness surrounding Laura and Manly. Laura recovered from her illness, but Manly suffered a stroke, most likely from trying to resume work too quickly while he was so weak. As a result, he would walk with a limp for the rest of his life, and often struggled with the dexterity in his hands. He was a young man, but would walk with a cane from then on.

Laura and Manly were strong people, but the hardships just kept piling up. In August 1889, Laura had a baby boy, but he died less than two weeks later. Grace's diary recorded the tragic event: "Laura's little baby boy . . . died a little while ago, he looked just like Manly." Then, to top it all off, the

Rose Wilder wears a formal lace collar and cuffs in this portrait, taken when she was about two-and-a-half.

Laura and Manly posed in wide-brimmed hats for this picture in sunny Florida.

couple's house burned down. Rose may have caused the fire while trying to help her grief-stricken mother by stoking the kitchen fire with hay sticks. The memory would stay with Rose: "I quite well remember watching the house burn, with everything we owned in the world, and knowing that I had done it."

It was time for a major change. Manly's father now had a thriving farm in Spring Valley, Minnesota. In the spring of 1890, Manly, Laura, and Rose left De Smet to go and live with Manly's parents for a while, helping out as best they could on the farm and concentrating on Manly's recovery. But after a year or so, Manly had not improved. There was talk that perhaps a warmer climate might help heal his partially paralyzed legs.

Laura's cousin Peter Ingalls had moved to southern Florida. In October 1891, the Wilder family boarded a train to visit him. Unfortunately, the sun did not seem to make a bit of difference when it came to Manly's legs. In addition,

Laura did not feel welcome or safe in Florida, and she disliked the humid climate.

"We went to live in the piney woods of Florida," she later wrote, "where the trees always murmur, where the butterflies are enormous, where plants that eat insects grow in moist places, and alligators inhabit the slowly moving waters of the rivers. But at that time and in that place, a Yankee woman was more of a curiosity than any of these." In August 1892, Laura, Manly, and Rose took the train back to De Smet. Laura was more than happy to leave Florida.

Laura sat for this portrait in the early years of her marriage.

The Wilders rented a house in town near Laura's family. It must have offered some relief to Laura to be with her sisters again. Mary had graduated from the college for the blind and was living with her parents and taking good care of their house. Carrie was working at the newspaper office, setting type, and Grace was in school.

The Ingalls family pictured, left to right, are: Caroline, Carrie, Laura, Charles, Grace, and Mary.

Rose remembered her family's new house less than fondly: "We had no furniture . . . there was only a cookstove and a big box for a table, Papa's and Mama's trunks, and their big bed and my little bed lying on the bare floors. . . . the wind had a different sound around that house, it sounded mean and jeering."

The Wilders kept busy in town. Rose started school at just five years old, having shown signs that she was eager to go and ready to learn. Laura worked long hours sewing for

Carrie Ingalls (standing in the doorway) worked in this printshop, which published De Smet's newspaper.

a dressmaker, "from six o'clock to six o'clock every day but Sunday." And Manly found odd jobs around town.

However, if the young family had any thoughts of making another go at farming, they were ruled out by persistent droughts. And things only got worse when the Panic of 1893 struck. People across the nation were being hard hit financially. Thousands of prairie farmers left the region in search of better lives. Laura and Manly still wanted to farm, but in a greener place. They started trying to save enough money to start a new farm elsewhere.

The Panic of 1893

In 1893, there was a nationwide economic depression. Severe droughts west of the Mississippi River had taken a huge toll on farms. The country had prospered in the past several years, but now companies had taken on too much debt, and were in trouble. One of the largest railroad companies, Reading Railroad, failed. It set off a domino effect. Soon, other railroad companies went out of business, the stock market lost value, prices of agricultural products such as wheat fell significantly, and people panicked. When people started pulling their money out of banks, some banks failed, too. The economy did not start to improve for four years.

After hearing news from former neighbors who had gone to live in Missouri's Ozark Mountains, the Wilders decided to try their luck there. Laura had managed to save $100, a considerable sum at the time. On July 17, 1894, Laura, Manly, and Rose left De Smet—and the Ingalls family— behind them.

chapter 9
A New Page

With Laura's $100 bill hidden away in a secret compartment in her writing desk, Manly, Laura, and seven-year-old Rose set out for Missouri. Laura warned Rose that she could never tell anyone about the money—it was their future, and they couldn't risk it getting lost or stolen. Another family, the Cooleys, came with them, traveling in their own wagon. The journey would take them through South Dakota, Nebraska, and Kansas, covering 650 miles (1046 km). It would be a long trip, but Laura helped Rose pass the time by telling stories about her childhood.

These two pioneer families, posing by their wagons, traveled in much the same way that the Wilders and Cooleys did in 1894.

Laura also began recording the story of her new life. She brought

This 1985 reenactment gives a sense of what a wagon train crossing the prairie looked like.

along a notebook to document the trip, using both sides of each page and fitting three lines of writing between each pair of ruled lines so she wouldn't waste any paper. One of her first entries noted the condition of the farms near De Smet: "Worst crops we have seen yet. No grass. Standing grain 3 inches high, burned brown and dead."

The weather during the Wilders' and Cooleys' trip was scorching hot—often over 100°F (38°C). To cool off and get clean, the families bathed in the river. Laura wrote about that, too: "Rose went out with Mrs. Cooley, she had a rope around her and I held onto its end."

Laura's entries include stories and descriptions of interesting people the group met along the way, towns they passed through, other wagons they ecountered, and crops they saw, such as corn and apples. At times, her sense of humor shines through: "I went to a house to buy milk. It was swarming with

> *"It is a drowsy country that makes you feel wide awake and alive but somehow contented."*
>
> —Laura

children and pigs; they looked a good deal alike." Throughout, her journal shows the mark of a true writer. Laura paid close attention to detail, and gave a full picture of her feelings and experiences. She also demonstrated her skill with words. Consider this beautiful passage: "It is a drowsy country that makes you feel wide awake and alive but somehow contented."

By August 3, 1894, the group had reached Lincoln, Nebraska, which Laura described as a "beautiful large city" with "grand buildings." Later, they passed through Topeka, Kansas, and saw automobiles and electric streetcars. They took a detour for a view of the capitol building there. On August 21, the wagons stopped in the town of Fort Scott, Kansas, to pick up letters from home. Along the way, the Wilders had also picked up a new passenger: a stray dog that they named "Fido" and kept as a pet.

There were times of boredom and discomfort: "We breathe dust all day and everything is covered thick with it." There were opportunities to enjoy the adventure: "We stopped by the road in the shade of trees and all of us had all the watermelon we could eat." Laura recorded it all.

Finally, the wagons passed into Missouri. "And the very first cornfield we saw beat even those Kansas cornfields,"

Laura wrote. Then, three days later: "Well, we are in the Ozarks at last, just in the beginning of them, and they are beautiful. . . . Manly says we could almost live on the looks of them." Clearly, both Manly and Laura liked what they saw.

In Springfield, Missouri, the Wilders bought new shoes for Rose, a dress for Laura, and a hat for Manly. Then on August 30, 1894, the wagons pulled into Mansfield, Missouri. "There is everything here already that one could want," declared Laura. This was the place. After so many days on the wagon, Rose was ecstatic to be able to run and play with the Cooley children.

Meanwhile, Manly and Laura looked for suitable land to buy. Laura soon fell in love with a place about one mile (1.6 km) from town. Rose later said that her mother "never had talked so fast." This land was "so much, much more than they'd hoped for. A year-round spring of the best water you ever drank,

Downtown Mansfield, Missouri, (pictured around 1900) featured tree-lined streets—and elevated wires to bring electricity to its residents.

a snug log house . . . four hundred young apple trees." And it was so close to a school that Rose could walk there.

Laura and Manly got dressed in their nicest clothes to go to the bank, where they would make payment on the property and sign papers for ownership. But when Laura went to retrieve the $100 bill from the secret spot in her writing desk, it was gone. Rose was in the hot seat. Her parents wanted to know if she had seen anyone near the desk, or if she had told anyone about the money. She hadn't.

It looked like the money was gone forever. This was a heavy blow to take, but Laura, who had gotten used to disappointment, soldiered on. And then, just as the terrible news of the lost money was

Manly and the horses that traveled with the family from De Smet pause in front of the Wilders' original Mansfield cabin.

sinking in, it was found! Somehow the bill had slipped into a crack in the desk, and Laura recovered it. In September 1894, Laura and Manly bought their new home. They named it Rocky Ridge Farm.

Twenty-seven-year-old Laura poses beside a pretty creek in this early photograph from Rocky Ridge.

Laura wanted to sweep the floors clean before they slept in their new home, so they planned to start cleaning out the cabin and spend their first night on the wagon. But when Manly lit the lantern, he found a strange man inside the house. The man was hungry, and was looking to find food—or work so he could buy food—for his wife and five children. Even though there was little to spare, Manly gave the man some salted pork and cornmeal and told him to come around the next day to help chop wood. Laura and Rose spent the next few days cleaning out the cabin and unpacking their things from the wagon. Manly and the stranger chopped firewood to sell in town.

The Wilders cleared the land, sowed seeds in the garden, sold eggs from their hens or traded them for supplies, and planted more apple trees. As they worked, Laura told Rose more stories from her childhood. Rose got to know the stories so well she could fill in the missing parts. Laura

Rose's favorite pet was a donkey named Spookendyke.

and Manly functioned as partners, working side by side, and Manly said he "would rather have [her] help than any man he ever sawed with." Laura later said: "The garden, my hens and the wood I helped saw and which we sold in town took us through the first year." It was hard work, but the Wilders finally seemed to be in a place where a successful lifestyle was within reach.

When school started at the new four-room brick schoolhouse in town, Rose dutifully attended. Sometimes she rode there on her pet donkey, Spookendyke. Rose was a quick study and, like her mother years earlier, often won the spelling bees held by the school. She loved most subjects and borrowed books from the library to continue her reading at home.

Although she was an excellent student, it was hard to be the new girl at school, especially when she was considered a poor "country girl." The girls who lived in town had pretty clothes and extra money for candy. They didn't want to sit with Rose, who instead had to share her desk with "the horrid, snuffling, unwashed, barefooted mountain girls." She often ate her lunch alone, with the company of only a book. Perhaps as a way of coping with her sense of being an outsider, Rose invented her own language. She called it "Fispooko" and would sometimes speak it to her donkey.

Rose found comfort at home, listening to her mother read stories aloud in the evenings. She later wrote: "Winter evenings were cozy in the cabin. The horses were warm in the little barn, the hens in the new wooden coop. . . . I sat on the floor, carefully building a house of corncobs, and my mother sat by the table, knitting needles flashing while she knitted warm woolen socks for my father and read to us from a book propped under the kerosene lamp."

Unfortunately, not all of Rose's memories were so pleasant. She knew what it felt like to be poor. "Because I loved my parents I would not let them suspect that I was suffering. I concealed from them how much I felt their poverty, their struggles and disappointments." Rose understood the truth—that although her family was poised to do well at Rocky Ridge, it was still going to take a lot of hard work before things got significantly better.

Laura probably took this photograph around 1910. It shows Rocky Ridge after Manly had cleared some of the land.

chapter **10**
Life on Rocky Ridge

The farm work was hard, but rewarding. And as the country recovered from the Panic of 1893, so did the Wilders. Rose helped churn butter and pick berries, both of which were taken to town to sell. They planted corn and potatoes, too. Laura learned all she could about hens and before long she was known for getting them to lay eggs better than any birds around. Manly, who had always been good with horses, started to breed Morgan horses.

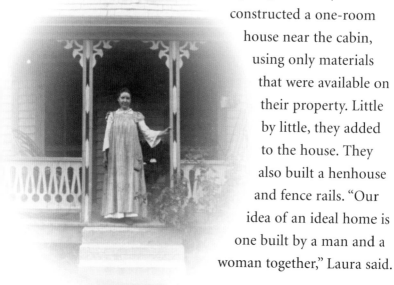

Laura stands on the porch of her little house in the town of Mansfield.

Laura and Manly also worked on building a new house for their family. Together, they constructed a one-room house near the cabin, using only materials that were available on their property. Little by little, they added to the house. They also built a henhouse and fence rails. "Our idea of an ideal home is one built by a man and a woman together," Laura said.

Manly worked hard to prepare the fields at Rocky Ridge for planting.

After several years, Rocky Ridge was thriving. Manly said: "When I look around the farm now and see the . . . good fields of corn and wheat and oats, when I see the orchard and strawberry fields like huge bouquets in the spring or full of fruit later in the season . . . I can hardly bring back to my mind the rough, rocky, brushy, ugly place that we first called Rocky Ridge Farm." Of course, it had never looked ugly to Laura. She had had a vision for the place since the moment she laid eyes on it.

In 1898, the Wilders decided to rent a house in town while continuing to build Rocky Ridge up into a farm that could turn a profit. Manly's father later gave them enough money to buy the house they were renting. Rose liked living in town and must have appreciated

MORGAN HORSES

Morgan horses were one of the earliest horse breeds in the United States, named for breeder Justin Morgan.

Laura may have taken this early picture of the Rocky Ridge farm.

some of the niceties it afforded a young girl. "In a few years we were not so poor," she remembered when she was older. But she still had trouble making friends. "I was too shy, too sensitive. . . . I was not invited to parties; I was 'left out.' I was hurt and lonely." It should be noted that most of what we know about Rose's childhood at Rocky Ridge is from Rose's point of view. While Laura didn't write much about this time of her daughter's life, Rose wrote a lot about her days growing up on the farm.

Laura and Manly continued to add to the farm. Eventually, the original 40-acre farm grew to 200 acres, and they enjoyed every bit of it. And the one-room house grew and grew, until it reflected the vision Laura had for it right from the start. One thing she knew she wanted was a lot of windows, to frame the "landscapes of forest and meadow and hills curving against the sky." There was even a window in the kitchen for Laura to gaze out of while she cooked or baked. Rose observed: "She hates kneading bread. . . . So the window is there. She forgets the kneading in looking at the sheep pasture."

There was also a dining room, a screened-in porch, a sitting room, a study, and three bedrooms. Oak beams that Laura and Manly had made with their own hands lined the ceiling. They even made a fireplace with stones they gathered around Rocky Ridge. By the time they were finished, they had built themselves a 10-room home. Laura was a contented woman. But even the most contented of people experience life's sorrows.

In the summer of 1902, Charles Ingalls—Laura's Pa—was dying. Laura took the train back to De Smet to see him one last time. He died on June 8, 1902. Pa's fiddle had played the soundtrack of Laura's childhood, and when he died he left her the beloved instrument. That trip to De Smet was also the last time Laura saw her mother and her sister Mary. She did not return for her mother's funeral in 1924, although she wrote of her sadness at her passing: "Darkness overshadowed the spring

> *"An ideal home is one built by a man and a woman together."*
>
> —Laura

Eliza Jane Wilder was Manly's sister, and had been Laura's teacher back in De Smet.

sunshine; a sadness crept into the bird's songs."

In 1903, 16-year-old Rose went to live for a year with Manly's older sister Eliza Jane (or "E.J.") in Crowley, Louisiana. E.J. was an intelligent, headstrong, and capable woman, and Laura had known her years before, when she was one of E.J.'s pupils in De Smet. Although Laura had not liked E.J. much, time had lessened their differences. It seemed E.J. recognized a kindred spirit in the complicated girl who was Rose.

Rose had grown into somewhat of a handful. She was very smart but had begun to dislike school. She had trouble getting along with the teachers, and often skipped class. Instead of going to school, she would stay at home and study math and history, and read all types of literature.

Rose would now attend the school in Crowley, which went beyond what the Mansfield school offered. Her Mansfield school records were so incomplete that the Crowley school required Rose to be tested in several subjects, including history, literature, civics, Latin, algebra, and geometry. She did well on all but the Latin and geometry exams, and agreed to study those subjects diligently. A year later, she finished at the top of her class in Latin. She even found time for a boyfriend, probably the first time she had dated. Rose wrote: "He drove me to school every morning . . . Every evening after school he was waiting for me." Rose also got involved with politics, encouraged by E.J., who was supporting Eugene Debs for president. It seems, however, that Rose may still have been an outsider among her peers. One fellow student later recalled: "Rose Wilder . . . cared only about her art and writing."

In any case, Rose was a much more confident person now. She wanted independence, and was ready to strike out on her own. With Laura's blessing, she learned to use a telegraph machine and took a job in Kansas City, leaving home at 17 to work for herself. Rose was soon earning $60 dollars a month, a huge sum at the time. And she had no trouble figuring out how to spend it. She liked high fashion, eating in restaurants, and generally being a "bachelor girl."

Rose, at 17 years old, poses for her graduation picture in Crowley, Louisiana.

chapter **11**

The Writing Life Begins

While Laura and Manly continued to make improvements at Rocky Ridge, they also worked in town to make extra money. Manly had a small hauling business and later delivered oil for a local company. With the second house so near the railroad station, Laura sold meals to the travelers who passed through town. But in 1910, the Wilders sold the house in town so they could be at the farm full-time. The developing orchards and the dairy cows required more attention. They also simply preferred to be there, enjoying their dream house.

By April 1908, Rose had moved to San Francisco, California, after briefly returning

Laura and Manly visit with friends on the porch at Rocky Ridge.

home to Rocky Ridge from Kansas City the year before. Laura and Rose wrote each other often. Rose's reasons for moving to San Francisco might have included a man named Gillette Lane, whom she had met while working as a telegraph operator in Kansas City. Lane was a newspaper reporter for the *San Francisco Call.* Rose married him on March 24, 1909, and became Rose Wilder Lane. She was 22 years old.

Soon after, the couple went back to Missouri. Their new life was quickly saddened, though, by the death of a baby son. Rose only mentions this twice, in letters to friends. She went to Rocky Ridge that summer.

Laura is dressed up for town in this 1906 photograph, featuring a fur coat and feathered hat.

In 1910, Rose began writing articles and essays for the *Kansas City Post.* The following year, the couple returned to California. Rose and Gillette became real-estate agents, and Rose was one of the first female agents in California. They did well in this business and bought a fast, red motorcar that Rose adored. It was "a purely wonderful car, the pride

of the town, the admiration of the highways."

Laura, too, started publishing some writing after Rose left home. Writing under the name of Mrs. A.J. Wilder, she had a small piece about hens printed in the *St. Louis Star Farmer* in 1910. Then, on February 18, 1911, she had an essay about country life published in the *Missouri Ruralist*.

Laura and Manly worked at Rocky Ridge for years to create a home that was suited to them in every detail. Even the low ceiling heights were designed for their proportions.

The *Ruralist* soon asked Laura to write more articles on farming and other topics. She was a natural writer, with a good sense of dialogue and setting. She knew how to make her stories come alive. Many of the letters between Rose and Laura at this time indicated that Rose was giving her mother advice about writing, and that they even discussed Laura's desire to write about her childhood.

For four years, Laura had occasional pieces published in the *Ruralist*. Then the paper got a new editor named John Case. He wanted the paper to have a "friendly, interesting, and personable style." Laura fit that profile perfectly, and Case began to use her more often. Eventually, she became a regular contributor to the paper, which had quite a large circulation. She sometimes shared her home-based beauty tips ("washing in buttermilk will whiten the hands and face") and thoughts about women's issues in her pieces. In one, she wrote: "It used to be that only the women in town could have the advantages of women's clubs, but now the woman in the country can be just as cultured a club woman as though she lived in town." Later, Laura began contributing to a few other newspapers as well. She wrote about life in the Ozarks for the *Kansas City Star* and the *St. Louis-Post Dispatch*. Laura often sent Rose her columns to read.

This picture of Manly by his apple trees was featured with one of Laura's articles for the *Missouri Ruralist*.

NEW YORK ☆ JOURNAL

House by a Vote of 373 to 50 Passes Joint Resolution

WAR IS DECLARED BY U. S.

Interned German Ships Seized by Customs Authorities

The United States officially entered World War I in 1917. But the effects had been felt in America since the war began in 1914.

The house at Rocky Ridge was finally finished in 1913. Laura adored it and remarked: "The effect is particularly good in summer when all the doors are open, making all the different parts of the house a harmonious whole." Laura and Manly were enjoying their life, despite the fact that money was still a bit tight. In 1913, they went to the Mansfield fair, and Manly won a prize for the best steer. The year after that, they won prizes for their chickens and cow. The local newspaper reported: "A.J. Wilder's prize-winning Durham cow gives 50 pounds of milk daily."

When World War I broke out in Europe in 1914, people began saving more and spending less. The real estate market fell off, and Rose and Gillette were no longer living the high life. They sold their fancy car and moved into a smaller apartment. Their marriage was also in trouble. Rose left her job as a real-estate agent and became a reporter and essayist for the *San Francisco Bulletin* in 1915.

Rose encouraged her mother to branch out from local newspapers and write for national magazines. She also arranged for a few of Laura's "children's verses" to be published in the *Bulletin*. It was the first time Laura had used the name Laura Ingalls Wilder in print. Rose was also beginning to write in new styles. She began to write serialized fiction stories for the *Bulletin,* and then biographies as well. She even interviewed the famous automobile giant Henry Ford, publishing "Henry Ford's Own Story" in the *Bulletin* in 1915, and as a book two years later. Rose was making quite a name for herself as a writer, becoming known both locally and nationally.

By 1915, Rose Wilder Lane had a national reputation as a writer.

Although she enjoyed her success, Rose missed her mother; Laura and Rose had not seen each other since 1911. It had been too expensive to travel, and Rose hadn't had room in her old apartment for Laura to be comfortable. But Rose was making good money now, and she asked her mother to come for a nice, long visit. She wrote: "I simply can't stand being so homesick for you any more. You must plan to come out here. . . . You've simply GOT to, so let me hear no argument about it."

POST CARD

A. J. Wilder
Mansfield
Missouri

The exposition is simply wonderful
so beautiful in every way.
Monday I shall see the Dogs of
Love Bessie

Laura sent this postcard to Manly from San Francisco, describing the "simply wonderful" exposition.

Manly had to stay behind and mind the farm, but Laura set out for California.

Rose made sure that it wouldn't be a hardship on her parents by paying Laura's train fare. She even gave Laura some money to make up for what the farm might lose in her absence. Rose explained to her mother: "I will be able to send you the fare, and while you are here and maybe right along afterward I can send you $5 a week to make up for what you will lose in chickens, etc., by the trip." This may also have been Rose's way of paying her parents back for a $250 loan they had given her.

Laura left Mansfield for California on August 21, 1915. She started what would become

Laura loved the views of San Francisco Bay, with its ferry boats crossing the wide water.

a long series of letters to Manly while still on the train. Laura made friends easily along the way, but her affection for Manly shines through in her letters: "I wish you were here. Half the fun I lose because I am all the time wishing for you."

Even though she missed Manly, Laura's visit with Rose in San Francisco was a wonderful adventure. It also seemed to have a profound effect on how she saw herself as a writer. Rose encouraged her mother, gave her advice, and helped her whenever she

West from Home

Laura loved to chronicle the major events in her life. When she and Manly made the journey from De Smet to Mansfield, she kept a journal noting everything that made an impression on her. In San Francisco, she took similar notes in the form of letters sent back to Manly. In this way, she could share the experience of visiting their daughter, as well as the many new sights and sounds of San Francisco and the World's Fair. Later, when Laura was a famous author, her letters from this trip were published in a book called *West from Home*.

could. When Rose was asked to send stories to a magazine in the East, she suggested that Laura take the job instead, telling her mother that the job "would probably pay $50 or so. . . . When you get things to running so that the farm work won't take up so much time you can do things like that."

Throughout the trip, Laura wrote to Manly about the many new sights and sounds that greeted her. "At Land's End I had my first view of the Pacific Ocean. To say it is beautiful does not half express it. . . . The water is such a deep wonderful blue and the sound of the waves breaking on the beach and their whisper as they flow back is something to dream about." Laura could not resist the pull of the ocean. "We went nearer the shore and dug holes in the sand with our toes. Went out to meet the waves and ran back before the big one caught us . . . just to think, the same water that bathes the shores of China and Japan came clear across the ocean and bathed my feet."

San Francisco enchanted her. "Set on the hills as it is with glimpses of the bay here and there . . . lights shining up and down the hills

An aerial view shows most of the "palaces" and halls at the Panama-Pacific International Exposition.

and the lights of ships on the water, it is like fairyland."

Laura also told Manly how she visited the *Bulletin* offices with Rose, and how their daughter was giving her pointers: "I do want to do a little writing with Rose to get the hang of it a little better." "Rose and I are blocking out a story of the Ozarks for me to finish when I get home. . . . If I can only get started at that, it will sell for a good deal more than farm stuff."

The main attraction in San Francisco that year was a world's fair called the Panama-Pacific International Exposition.

The World's Fair

The 1915 Panama-Pacific International Exposition was a world's fair celebrating the newly completed Panama Canal, and San Francisco's recovery from a devastating 1906 earthquake. Every U.S. state and nearly every nation in the world was represented, and millions attended. The fair spanned 635 acres, including temporary "palaces" such as the 43-feet- (13-m-) tall Tower of Jewels, which glittered with more than 100,000 cut-glass "jewels."

Laura and Rose spent a great deal of time exploring the many exhibits. In October, the *Missouri Ruralist* asked Laura to write a few articles about the exposition for the paper back home. One such article appeared on that paper's front page on December 5, 1915. Slowly but surely, Laura was making a name for herself as a writer.

chapter **12**

Rose Returns to Rocky Ridge

aura's last letter to Manly from California was mailed from San Francisco on October 22, 1915. Soon afterward, Laura boarded a train for Rocky Ridge. When she arrived home, she settled happily back into her routine on the farm, taking care of the house, the gardens, the chickens, and Manly.

For the next nine years, Laura also wrote articles for the *Ruralist* almost every week. Her early columns were straightforward pieces about agricultural topics and life at Rocky Ridge. Over time, she wrote more far-reaching stories that often included lessons about becoming a better person. She wrote about current events and politics, and increasingly wove into her stories personal details about her pioneer childhood—anecdotes

This photograph of Laura was taken in 1906.

that would later find their way, in fictional form, into her books.

One area of particular interest to Laura and her readers was the ongoing war in Europe. World War I was at the forefront of people's minds, especially after April 6, 1917, when the United States entered the war. Laura shared her thoughts through her column in the *Ruralist*. In a May 1918 piece, she wrote: "We are in the midst of a battle of standards of conduct and each of us is a soldier in the ranks. . . .

Laura did her writing at this desk at Rocky Ridge. Today, the desk is preserved and displayed at the Laura Ingalls Wilder Historic Home and Museum in Mansfield.

We may have thought that . . . a disregard of the rights of others for our own advantage, did not matter so much. . . . Nevertheless it is these same things when done in mass by the German government and armies, that the remainder of the world abhors."

In some cases, Laura's column showcased the ideals of people who stood for justice, as well as criticizing the behavior of those who were not acting in the best interests of the nation. In a column from July 1918, she spoke of an unnamed man: "I knew of one person in the recent Red Cross drive who bought as cheaply as possible . . . and resold at a profit. There were only a few dollars involved but there was the soul of a profiteer in a person who . . . is just as obnoxious as the man who makes millions out of the suffering of the world." In sharp contrast, she noted: "Not far from this man lives another who served in the U.S. army . . . He is entitled to a pension but . . . would not ask for a pension until this mess was straightened out and the government expenses were lighter."

The equality of women was another issue on people's minds at the time. In many parts of the country, there were marches and parades in support of the cause. Of course, Laura believed in the equal partnership between a man and a wife, and this theme often cropped up in her writing. Toward the end of her tenure at the *Ruralist*, her column ran with the overall title "As a Farm Woman Thinks."

Laura had become more active in the Mansfield community, too. She helped start the Athenians, a women's study club that met to talk about literature, and founded the first county library. When the Mansfield Farm Loan Association was formed in 1917 to help farmers get

By LAURA INGALLS WILDER

In January 1925, Laura published this article in *The Country Gentleman*.

loans and expand their businesses, Laura became its secretary-treasurer.

By 1918, Rose and Gillette were divorced, but Rose continued writing full-time under the name Rose Wilder Lane. She also continued to advise her mother about the columns she was writing. At one point, Rose suggested that Laura revise some of Rose's stories and sell them as her own. "I have just finished writing a very fair story of how a certified-milk dairy is run . . . it is very interesting stuff. I thought if you could get some local names to hang it upon you might resell my stuff bodily for say, the . . . *Ruralist*, or perhaps to the *Kansas City Star*."

Rose also sometimes drew on stories from her mother's life. She used some of the people and events described in Laura's memoir "Pioneer Girl" in two short stories of her own. And much later, Rose based *Let the Hurricane Roar* on what she knew of Laura's parents, Charles and Caroline, and their lives as pioneers. Of course, Rose had plenty of her own material to work with—her novel *Diverging Roads*, published in 1919,

The Women's Suffrage Movement

The movement for women's suffrage—the right to vote—was first started in America by Elizabeth Cady Stanton in 1848, when she organized the Seneca Falls Convention. Over the ensuing decades, Stanton, Susan B. Anthony, and many other women worked tirelessly for this cause. From the early 1900s until 1920—when the Nineteenth Amendment finally prohibited the government from denying any citizen the right to vote due to gender—women participated in marches and protests fighting for their rights.

was about the troubles a woman faced juggling her career and her marriage.

In 1918, after visiting Rocky Ridge, Rose moved to New York City for a while. She worked as a book doctor, helping other writers improve their work, while continuing to publish her own. From afar, Rose continued to encourage her mother to send stories to magazines and other national publications. Rose herself had already been published in *Sunset* and *McCall's,* two popular and respected national magazines. "There is no reason under heaven why you should not be making four or five thousand dollars a year," she told her mother. Soon, she helped land Laura an assignment for *McCall's,* which Rose edited for her. This marked the beginning of a professional relationship that would later lead to Rose helping Laura with her book manuscripts. Laura's article—entitled "Whom Will You Marry?"—ran in the June 1919 issue.

Rose enjoyed her travels abroad. This picture is from her time in France.

Rose knew her mother had great potential and held her to as high a standard as she did herself and the other professional writers with whom she worked. When Laura turned in a second article, Rose took her to task: "I don't think you have quite done it yet." As Laura continued to explore her writing and began to work on stories about her childhood, Rose helped her hone her skills. She encouraged Laura to write more in the way she spoke and taught her the classic "show, don't tell" rule of writing: "Don't say those things were so, show that they were so. Your log cabin in the Great Woods . . . your trip through Kansas . . . the building of the railroad through the Dakotas . . . Make the reader see it with his eyes." They were crucial lessons to learn on the road to becoming a great writer.

In the summer of 1919, Rose returned to Rocky Ridge and stayed on through September. Then the following spring, in May 1920, she traveled to Europe, employed as a writer for the Red Cross, the international aid organization. While overseas, Rose wrote articles as well as children's stories for the Junior Red Cross magazine. With her popularity as a writer growing, Rose was in good spirits. In her diary, she wrote: "I feel simply brimming over with stories."

While Rose was in Europe, she and Laura exchanged many letters, keeping

Rose's travels took her to Egypt, where she stood before the great pyramids.

each other up to date on what was going on in their lives. Rose's years in Europe had not been without difficulties, and for a time, she had suffered from illness. Then, in December 1923, Rose returned to Rocky Ridge. "Like a dream, Mama Bess [Rose's nickname for Laura] met me at Mansfield Station." But just weeks later, she wrote in her diary: "This life is almost intolerable."

Rose was not suited to the farming lifestyle, but for some reason it seems she felt obligated to stay. "My mother is old and not very well, and wants me to stay here," she wrote to a friend. But Laura was actually only 57 years old at the time and seems to have been in fine health. By springtime, Rose felt a bit more contented, and spent time working on her own writing projects as well as helping out on the farm. In the fall, she left once more, but with plans to return to Rocky Ridge in the future.

In January 1925, Rose was back in Mansfield, after receiving word from Laura that she

Laura and Rose pose with Isabelle the car during their 1925 road trip.

Rose built this stone house for her parents at Rocky Ridge. In addition to being beautiful, it was also more modern than the old farmhouse.

was not well. This time, Rose's friend Helen Boylston—a nurse she had met in Europe—accompanied her. Rose had earned enough money to buy a slightly used blue Buick, which caused quite a stir in sleepy Mansfield. She named the car Isabelle. That September, Rose, Laura, and Helen took a car trip together and went exploring. Over the course of six weeks, they drove all the way to California and back.

Rose left Rocky Ridge in 1926, but returned in 1928. She had earned a good sum of money for her work in *The Country Gentleman* and wanted to build a new house for her parents—"a darling cottage . . . done in field stone . . . with brick window-sills and a tiny bit of a brick terrace." She also had the old house wired for electricity and made major improvements to the plumbing. On Christmas Day, 1928, Rose gave her parents the key to their new home.

chapter **13**

A Mother-Daughter Arrangement

When Rose first started editing her mother's magazine articles, there was often some discussion about Rose's heavy-handed rewrites. For example, when Rose edited Laura's first *McCall's* piece, she told her mother: "Don't be absurd about my doing the work on your article. I didn't re-write it a bit more than I rewrite Mary Heaton Vorse's articles." If Laura's feathers were ruffled, they may have been calmed by her daughter's compliment: "At least your copy was all the meat of the article."

While Rose was having the stone house built for her parents, she also had electricity put in the farmhouse.

By 1925, Laura's interest in writing her life story was growing.

And in 1930, even though money was scarce, Laura turned her full attention to the project that had been lingering in her mind for so long. She wrote a full draft of her autobiography and titled it "Pioneer Girl." During this time, Rose and Laura were living in the two houses at Rocky Ridge. It was easy for Laura to simply walk her work over to Rose when she was ready. Two things seem clear—Rose edited the manuscript, but Laura was not shy about speaking up if she was not happy with the proposed changes. The story was simply too close to her heart.

Rose sent Laura's book to her agent, who in turn submitted it to publishers in hope of a book deal. While it received praise from some publishers, the nonfiction manuscript was rejected by all of them. One publisher said, "If the same material were used as a basis for a fiction serial they'd take it like a shot." Rose soon hired a new agent, George Bye. When she sent "Pioneer Girl" to him, he said, "It didn't seem to have enough high points or crescendo. . . . A fine old lady was sitting in a rocking chair and telling a story chronologically but with no benefit of perspective or theatre." Still, he submitted it to publishers. Once again, it was rejected.

The evidence was mounting that Laura might need to rethink "Pioneer Girl" and consider making it a work of fiction. And her thinking took yet another new direction when Rose met with a children's book editor who was interested in the subject matter. "I like the material you have used, it covers a period in American history about

One of the inexpensive tablets Laura preferred for writing her books by hand.

which very little has been written, and almost nothing for boys and girls," editor Marion Fiery said.

Laura began to change her autobiography into a children's story about a girl named Laura, based on the facts of her life. She later said: "The book is not a history but a true story founded on historical fact." She set to work adding descriptions of pioneer life, and setting up the structure of the story so that it followed a calendar year in the life of the fictional Laura. Some things that had happened in her life were left out either because they did not make for a good story, or they were not appropriate for a children's book. For example, Laura chose not to include the death of her younger brother, Freddie, in any of her novels. She explained to Rose: "It does not belong in the picture I am making of the family."

Rose and Laura had a complicated relationship, as many mothers and daughters do—especially those who share a common interest. And of course, they saw the world in different ways. While Rose sought adventure and travel,

Laura preferred to stay at home. And while Rose could be headstrong and brooding, Laura seemed more matter-of-fact and calm. Like many mothers and daughters, their opinions of each other were sometimes clouded. For instance, Rose saw her mother as her writing pupil, and a less worldly person than she was.

But Laura had strong talents of her own as a writer, and a complex

The letter from Laura's agent George Bye, confirming the sale of her first book.

understanding of the world even though she didn't travel much. She was a smart businesswoman and even ran for the public office of collector in her county.

> "The material you have used . . . covers a period in American history about which very little has been written."
>
> —Marion Fiery, children's book editor, in response to "Pioneer Girl"

Some remembered their relationship as strained. The Wilders' neighbor Roscoe Jones recalled: "Mother and daughter were not so close, I think. . . . [Rose] wasn't nearly as easy to visit with as her

Laura and Rose enjoy a walk beside a stream at Rocky Ridge farm.

mother because she seemed so brash." Of course, the townspeople of Mansfield, Missouri, had their own reasons for not seeing Rose in the best light. In 1935, Rose had published a collection of short stories called *Old Home Town,* based on people from Mansfield—and most did not appreciate how they were portrayed in the book.

However, there is no doubt that there was a strong connection between Rose and Laura. And as historian Stephen Hines notes, "It is a testimony to the strength of family ties that mother and daughter came through their six or seven years of close proximity, collaborating and competing over the same material, with their relationship still intact."

As an author in her own right, working on her mother's writing was probably hard for Rose at times. Between the time she spent on her mother's manuscripts and the writing projects

". . . as soon as I can get through this work that's piled up ahead of me, I'll really write a beautiful thing."

—Rose Wilder Lane

she took on to earn money, Rose was frustrated by the slow progress of her own writing career. Like many writers, Rose had good years and lean years. And in a letter to a friend, she wrote: "I somehow always have the idea that as soon as I can get through this work that's piled up ahead of me, I'll really write a beautiful thing."

Still, throughout the years, Rose continued working on her mother's books with her. And as in any close working relationship, there were disagreements. In one of Laura's later novels, it seemed Rose thought her mother should change some points in the storyline. While Laura did not necessarily agree, she told Rose, "I have written you the whys of the story as I wrote it. But you know your judgment is better than mine, so what you decide is the one that stands."

By December 1931, Laura's revisions were finished. In the meantime, due to business reasons that had nothing to do with Laura, the book was now in the hands of a new editor at Harper & Brothers. Her first book was to be called *Little House in the Big Woods.*

chapter **14**

From Farmer to Award-Winning Author

In the summer of 1931, while the manuscript was in the hands of Laura's editor, Laura and Manly took a trip to De Smet. On June 10, there was to be an Old Settlers' Day celebration, and they wanted to be there. They traveled back over much of the same route they had taken when moving to Mansfield from De Smet all those years ago. Laura hadn't visited the town since her father died in 1902, and Manly hadn't been back at all.

Along the way, the Wilders stopped to visit Laura's sister Grace, then traveled to the town of Keystone,

Laura and Manly's travels took them to the Black Hills of South Dakota, where Mount Rushmore was still under construction.

South Dakota, to see her sister Carrie. (Mary had died in 1928.) "Grace seems like a stranger only now and then something familiar about her face," Laura wrote in her diary. "It all makes me miss those who are gone, Pa and Ma and Mary and the Boasts and Cap Garland."

This postcard shows the local school in Malone, New York, where Manly lived when he was young.

Once the couple reached De Smet, the memories continued to flood back. Laura described standing "nearly in the place where Carrie and I walked to school and Manly used to drive Barnum and Skip as he came dashing out to take me on those long Sunday afternoon drives when I was seventeen."

The trip made Laura nostalgic for her past. It brought back details of the life she and Manly led when they were young. Laura loved her husband very much and was proud of the man he had become. Having a book about her own early childhood, she decided to base her next book on Manly's childhood. It was called *Farmer Boy*. The first time Laura submitted the manuscript for *Farmer Boy*, it was rejected. But by the summer of 1933, it had been revised and accepted by her publisher. Rose even helped Laura by

By 1942 (when this picture was taken) Laura and Manly were enjoying a more relaxed life at Rocky Ridge, thanks to the proceeds from Laura's books.

traveling to Malone, New York, where Manly had grown up, and providing her with invaluable detailed information about the places from his childhood.

Meanwhile, in April 1932, when Laura was 65 years old, *Little House in the Big Woods* came out. It received rave reviews and was chosen by the Junior Literary Guild as its recommended selection that month. Despite the fact that the country was suffering another economic downturn, and people had less money to spend on non-essential items such as books, *Little House in the Big Woods* was an immediate success. It was followed by the publication of *Farmer Boy* in 1933.

Laura was on a roll. She started writing a third book, about her life on the Kansas prairie as a young girl. As she worked on the book, Rose wrote to her agent: "My mother is now doing another book about her childhood experiences among the Indians . . . promises to beat *Little*

House all hollow." *Little House on the Prairie* came out in 1935. The *New York Times* said: "Mrs. Wilder has caught the very essence of pioneer life, the satisfaction of hard work, the thrill of accomplishment, safety and comfort made possible through resourcefulness and exertion."

After that, Laura wrote about her family's time in Minnesota—leaving out the time they lived at the rowdy hotel in Burr Oak, Iowa, as well as the loss of her baby brother, which had happened shortly before. These are just two examples of how her fiction books varied from Laura's real life. Going from Walnut Grove to Burr Oak and back to Walnut Grove again would have been a fairly complicated storyline. Streamlining the events and leaving the Iowa interlude out made for a better plot.

Rose had moved to Columbia, Missouri, in July 1935, and then on to Connecticut, leaving Rocky Ridge behind. Laura and Manly moved from the rock cottage back into their beloved farmhouse. But Laura and Rose still found ways to work closely together, communicating back and forth during the revision of Laura's fourth book. Laura made maps and Rose asked questions, tugging at Laura's memories of people and places from so long ago. In response to some of her daughter's questions, Laura made the appropriate changes and responded: "I see

"Mrs. Wilder has caught the very essence of pioneer life."

—*New York Times*

the pictures so plainly that I guess I failed to paint them as I should."

At other times, Laura disagreed with Rose's edits. When Rose changed a sentence so that Ma "vowed she didn't believe those young ones were ever going to sleep," Laura replied that her mother was too proper to have called them "young ones." Overall, however, the collaboration went smoothly, and Laura's skills as a writer continued to sharpen. Her fourth book was called *On the Banks of Plum Creek* and was published in 1937. It was awarded a prestigious Newbery Honor from the American Library Association.

The first editions of Laura's Little House books featured illustrations by Helen Sewell and Mildred Boyle.

Laura now had a firmly rooted reputation as one of the best children's-book authors in the country. As a result, she was asked to speak at the national Book Week conference in Detroit in October 1937. She talked about the inspiration for the Little House books: "I wanted the children now to understand more about the beginning of things, to know what is behind the things they see—what it is that made America as they know it."

That year, thanks to the earnings from Laura's books, Laura and Manly had a comfortable income for the first time in their lives. Laura was aware of how much Rose had done along the way. "Without your help I would not have the royalties from my books in the bank to draw on," she told her daughter. In addition to the income, Laura began to receive something she had not anticipated: fan mail.

At 65, Laura had become instantly famous with *Little House in the Big Woods*—especially among the younger crowd. She received piles of adoring letters from children. One child wrote: "I would like to know if you have any more books like [*Little House*]. . . . I wish it would never come to an end." Laura said, "Children who read it wrote to me begging for more. I was amazed." She tried to answer them all.

Neta Seal, a Mansfield neighbor and friend of the Wilders, recalled: "Oh, Mrs. Wilder did get letters from schoolchildren, letters and letters and letters. At first, she answered each one individually . . . she got to where she'd just write the teacher a letter and let her read it to all the children." Another neighbor remembered: "Sometimes the mail would get to be too much and she'd have her hands full."

Laura also received letters from teachers, librarians, and parents. They told her about children who "read in the

Laura's fan mail flooded in from children as far away as Japan. On her 84th birthday, she received nearly 1,000 pieces of mail.

to hear from you.

Your friend,
Mary Ruth Cannon

94 N. Union St.
Concord, N.C.
Jan. 3, 1933

Dear Mrs. Wilder,
I am a little girl in the fifth grade. We are studying about books and authors. Each has chosen an author we is trying to find. We say about them. Your "Little House in the Woods." Will you tell me some thing your self? I found about you in young about you in young What other books you written? will be so happy

Fulton School
Mount Vernon, N.Y.
May 8, 1936

Dear Mrs Wilder:
I am one of the very fortunate children to have read your excellent book "Little House In the Big Woods." The part that interested me most was when Laura and Mary were going to town. It seemed very strange that the children would think it a great honor to go to town. The reason my class enjoyed hearing your book was because it was particularly about your childhood. Thank you for writing your lovely book. We would be very glad to have a reply from you.
Sincerely yours,
Helen Kaplan

bathtub, under the covers with flashlights, at the dinner table."

A letter from one librarian read, "We librarians are very grateful to you for giving us a series of books so fine and at the same time so appealing to children."

Laura soon began working on her fifth book, *By the Shores of Silver Lake.* With this book, she had a new challenge that she both recognized and accepted. As the fictional Laura grew up, the subject matter of the books was starting to be geared for slightly older readers. And it wasn't only the fictional Laura who was growing up—she had a dedicated fan base of readers who had been getting older with each subsequent book, as well. Rose was worried about this, but Laura was not. "I don't see how we can spare what you call adult stuff, for that makes the story," she wrote. Laura was now seasoned enough to trust her own instincts. *By the Shores of Silver Lake* came out in 1939, and Laura earned another Newbery Honor.

Next came *The Long Winter,* which was based on the experience of that first, hard winter in De Smet when the Ingalls family and the rest of the town nearly starved from lack of food. Dredging up those old memories was emotionally difficult for Laura. "It has been rather trying, living it all over again as I did in the writing of it, and I am glad it is finished," she wrote in a letter to her agent, George Bye.

The Long Winter was followed in 1941 by *Little Town on the Prairie,* which focused on Laura's teenage years, and then in 1943 by the story of Laura and Manly's first years as a married couple in *These Happy Golden Years.* And with these three books came three more Newbery Honors! She had written eight books in the series, which had now come to an end. Laura Ingalls Wilder was 76 years old.

This photograph shows Laura signing books for some of her young fans at a library.

chapter **15**

A Literary Legacy

With her last book finished, Laura was thrilled to have free time to spend enjoying life at Rocky Ridge with her husband. They gardened, took drives, and read. Manly continued to make fine pieces of furniture by hand. But there was no escaping the fact that Laura was also an internationally known author, receiving hundreds of letters each week from fans. People traveled from all over to meet her. Although these gestures were flattering, they often amounted to an invasion of privacy.

In 1949, Manly suffered a heart attack. He died on October 23, 1949, at the age of 92. He and Laura had been married for 64 years, and she was devastated. "I am very lonely," she wrote. "My heart is too sore to write more."

Laura was now an elderly woman, living on her own. Luckily, two neighbor boys named Sheldon and Roscoe Jones were there to help Laura around Rocky Ridge.

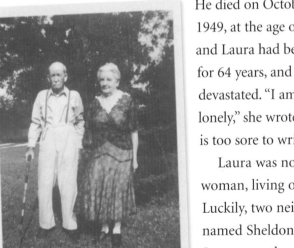

Laura and Manly stand together at Rocky Ridge in 1948.

They would take in the mail, rake leaves, and mow the lawn. Sheldon also helped ward off the many fans who would simply show up at Laura's house to see her. "There were always people coming by . . . wanting to meet her," he later recalled. "I don't know how many times I'd be working in the yard when I'd have to make a run for the back door to get between visitors and the house."

In 1949, Laura formally acknowledged all the help Rose had given her by arranging for Rose to receive 10 percent of the royalties from the Little House books. Laura wrote: "I owe Rose, for helping me, at first, in selling my books and for the publicity she gave them. . . . This arrangement should have been made long ago." In May of that same year, the Detroit Public Library honored Laura by naming a branch after her. One year later, the public library in Pomona, California, named its children's area the Laura Ingalls Wilder Room.

Often, the people from a person's hometown take longer to see one of their own in the same celebrity light that others do. This was true of Laura and the town of Mansfield. People there knew her as a farm wife, a newspaper columnist, and an active member of their community—but not as a famous author. Eventually, Mansfield caught up to the rest of the country. In 1951, the Mansfield library was renamed the Laura Ingalls Wilder Library. The ceremony, which was held in the high-school gym, featured a parade of schoolchildren. Laura wore a red velvet dress for the occasion.

In 1953, new illustrated editions of the Little House books were published. Illustrator Garth Williams had traveled to Rocky Ridge to meet Laura and see some of the people and places for himself as he prepared the new drawings for her books. The following year, the American Library Association created the Laura Ingalls Wilder Award, to be given each year to an American author who has made "a substantial and lasting contribution to literature for children." Laura was the first recipient of the bronze medal, which had been designed by Williams.

By early 1957, Laura's health was deteriorating. She had been diagnosed with diabetes a few months earlier. So she would not be alone at night in her weakened condition, a local woman named Virginia Hartley came to help Laura in the evenings, and also helped her with errands during the daytime. Virginia was there when Laura passed away, three days after her 90th birthday, on February 10, 1957. Her obituary read, "While the pencil of Mrs. Laura Ingalls Wilder, 90, has stopped with her death, the works of that pencil will live on forever."

That was most certainly true. After Laura's death, Rose inherited her mother's estate. Among Laura's papers, she found the diary that documented the 1894 move from De Smet to Mansfield. Rose took the unedited diary entries, added an introduction and an epilogue to help readers put Laura's writing

EPILOGUE

An epilogue is a concluding section that rounds out a literary work.

into context, and published the diary as *On the Way Home*. The book gave insight into a part of Laura's life that had not been previously well known.

In the years that followed, Rose remained a traveling, working writer. She died on October 30, 1968, at the age of 81, just as she was about to set out on a three-year trip around the world. Rose's heir was a man named Roger Lea MacBride, whom she had taken

Rose continued to work on her mother's writing even after Laura's death.

under her wing in the 1940s and thought of as a grandson.

After Rose's death, MacBride discovered the rough draft of a manuscript that Laura had written, but never revised, about the early years of her marriage. He sent it to Laura's publisher and in 1971—14 years after her death—*The First Four Years* was published. Since there aren't any diaries or letters from this time in Laura's life, it is tempting to look at *The First Four Years* as a record of what early married life was really like for Laura and Manly. However, like most of Laura's books, *The First Four Years* is a work of fiction—and an unedited one at that.

Three years later, in 1974, MacBride compiled the letters Laura had written during her 1915 trip to San Francisco. MacBride wrote: "Tumbled in a cardboard box along with old recipes, faded pictures, and newspaper clippings of persons and events long gone, I found these letters and postcards from Laura Ingalls Wilder to her husband, Almanzo." The result was another publication by Laura Ingalls Wilder entitled *West from Home.*

Also in 1974, MacBride became co-producer of a television series loosely based on Laura's Little House books. The popular *Little House on the Prairie* starred Melissa Gilbert as Laura and Michael Landon as Pa. It ran until 1983.

Today, important locations from the life of Laura Ingalls Wilder are maintained throughout the midwest. From Walnut Grove, Minnesota, to De Smet, South Dakota, these landmarks give fans insight into Laura's colorful real life and the times in which she lived. However, one such site might never have been established if it

The television show *Little House on the Prairie* introduced Laura's story to a whole new generation of fans.

Laura's humor and spirit live on in the books she wrote, the works she inspired, and the hearts of readers everywhere.

wasn't for some serious detective work. Consider the Kansas prairie where Charles Ingalls settled his family in 1869. Because he was on Osage Indian territory, there was no official claim; thus, no record of where exactly the homestead was. In 1977, a librarian named Margaret Clements solved the mystery.

Clements pieced together a map based on census reports and all the claims listed. Once she had pinpointed the probable site of the Ingalls cabin, she contacted the people who owned the land, 13 miles (21 km) southwest of Independence, Kansas. They showed her a hand-dug well that matched the location of a house in an atlas from that time. They had found it! Today, that spot is home to a reproduction of the cabin based on Laura's descriptions.

So, in museums, landmarks, and most especially her books—and as anyone who truly knew her could have predicted—Laura Ingalls Wilder's story lives on, a lasting legacy for young and old readers alike.

Events in the Life of Laura Ingalls Wild

February 1, 1860
Caroline Quiner marries
Charles Ingalls.

May 23, 1877
Grace Ingalls
is born.

August 3, 1870
Caroline Celestia
Ingalls is born.

Spring 1871
Ingallses move back
to Wisconsin.

January 10, 1865
Mary Amelia
Ingalls is born.

November 1, 1875
Charles Frederick
Ingalls is born.

December 10, 1883
Laura passes
teacher's
examination.

February 7, 1867
Laura Elizabeth
Ingalls is born.

February 1874
Ingallses move
to Walnut Grove,
Minnesota.

August 25, 1885
Laura Ingalls marries
Almanzo Wilder.

September 1869
Ingallses settle near
Independence, Kansas.

August 27, 1876
Charles Frederick
Ingalls dies.

December 5, 1886
Rose Wilder is born.

August 25, 1889
Laura has a baby boy
who dies soon after.

July 17, 1894
The Wilders leave De
Smet for Missouri.

April 1932
*Little House in the Big
Woods* is published.

October 23, 1949
Almanzo Wilder dies.

Summer 1931
Laura and Manly
visit De Smet.

October 30, 1968
Rose Wilder
Lane dies.

June 8, 1902
Charles Ingalls dies.

1953
New Garth Williams
illustrations are
made for the Little
House books.

September 1894
The Wilders buy
Rocky Ridge Farm.

August 1915
Laura visits Rose
in San Francisco.

February 10, 1957
Laura Ingalls
Wilder dies.

For Further Study

There are several museums and historic sites to visit and learn more about Laura Ingalls Wilder.

The Laura Ingalls Wilder Memorial Society, De Smet, South Dakota, was founded shortly after her death in 1957. At this site, is the surveyor's house that the Ingalls family live in for a time. http://www.liwms.com/

The Laura Ingalls Wilder Museum is in Walnut Grove, Minnesota, and has replicas of buildings from the time Laura's family lived there. Nearby, is the original site of the dugout where the Ingalls lived when they first arrived. The dugout is gone, but the spot has a marker with a description. http://www.walnutgrove.org/museum.htm

Southwest of Independence, Kansas, there is a reconstruction of a log cabin according to Laura's descriptions. http://www.littlehouseontheprairie.com/

In Burr Oak, Iowa, there is the Laura Ingalls Wilder Park and Museum. http://www.lauraingallswilder.us/

The Laura Ingalls Wilder Home and Historic Museum is at the Rocky Ridge Farm in Mansfield, Missouri. http://www.lauraingallswilder.us/

Almanzo Wilder's home is featured in the book Farmer Boy (<http://www.almanzowilderfarm.com/> http://www.almanzowilderfarm.com/). Tour the rebuilt barns and restored house.

Tanya Lee Stone www.tanyastone.com <http://www.tanyastone.com> **Elizabeth Leads the Way** (Holt, 2008) **Up Close: Ella Fitzgerald** (Viking, 2008) **Sandy's Circus** (Viking, 2008) **Almost Astronauts** (Candlewick, 2009) **Laura Ingalls Wilder** (DK, 2009) **A Bad Boy Can Be Good for a Girl** (Wendy Lamb/Random House) www.myspace.com/tanyaleestoneauthor <http://www.myspace.com/tanyaleestoneauthor>

Works Cited

P. 11: "Neighbors took turns…" Laura: The Life of Laura Ingalls Wilder, p. 16. **P. 12:** "Who would wish…" Laura Ingalls Wilder: A Biography, p. 31. **P. 16:** "a cook stove…" Laura Ingalls Wilder: A Writer's Life, p. 9. **P. 18:** "They stayed about…" Laura: The Life of Laura Ingalls Wilder, p. 40. **P. 18:** "sounded much worse…" Laura Ingalls Wilder: A Writer's Life, p. 12. **P. 19:** "An Indian came…" Laura: The Life of Laura Ingalls Wilder, p. 40. **P. 21:** "for days and days…" Laura Ingalls Wilder: A Writer's Life, p. 14. **P. 22:** "because Jack wanted…" Laura Ingalls Wilder: A Writer's Life, p. 10. **P. 23:** "little half pint…" and "mad dog" and "put his fingers…" Laura Ingalls Wilder: A Writer's Life, p. 15. **P. 24:** "I was a regular…" I Remember Laura, p. 68. **P. 27:** "We were all going…" Laura: The Life of Laura Ingalls Wilder, p. 72. **P. 27:** "pretty little book…" Laura Ingalls Wilder: A Writer's Life, p. 18. **P. 28:** "so close to the creek…" Laura Ingalls Wilder: A Writer's Life, p. 76. **P. 28:** "my ears hurt…" and "One night Mary…" Laura Ingalls Wilder: A Writer's Life, p. 19. **P. 29:** "The grass along the road…" Laura Ingalls Wilder: A Writer's Life, pp. 19-20. **P. 31:** "I was with her…" Laura Ingalls Wilder: A Writer's Life, p. 21. **P. 32:** "country girls" Laura Ingalls Wilder: A Biography, p. 54. **P. 33:** "Pa told us goodbye…" Laura Ingalls Wilder: A Writer's Life, p. 22. **P. 34:** "behind the church…" and "Coming home from school…" Laura Ingalls Wilder: A Writer's Life, p. 23. **P. 34:** "While the snow…" Laura: The Life of Laura Ingalls Wilder, p. 97. **P. 35:** "It terrified me…" Laura Ingalls Wilder: A Writer's Life, pp. 23-24. **P. 36:** "the ground looked…" Laura Ingalls Wilder: A Writer's Life, p. 22. **P. 37:** "Little Brother got worse…" Laura Ingalls Wilder: A Writer's Life, p. 26. **P. 37-38:** "it was not a new…" Laura Ingalls Wilder: A Writer's Life, p. 27. **P. 38:** "Pa and ma didn't like…" Laura Ingalls Wilder: A Writer's Life, p. 27. **P. 38:** "Steadman handled the money…" Laura Ingalls Wilder: A Writer's Life, p. 28. **P. 38-39:** "Even if it rained…" Laura Ingalls Wilder: A Writer's Life, p. 29. **P. 39:** "I have always…" and "Pa knew…" Laura: The Life of Laura Ingalls Wilder, p. 118. **P. 39:** "Her hair was golden…" Laura Ingalls Wilder: A Biography, p. 72. **P. 40:** "the rippling brook…" Laura: The Life of Laura Ingalls Wilder, p. 120. **P. 41:** "Everything came at us…" Laura Ingalls Wilder: A Biography, p. 76. **P. 42:** "Only one boy…" Laura: The Life of Laura Ingalls Wilder, p. 135. **P. 43:** "Pa could not get…" Laura Ingalls Wilder: A Writer's Life, p. 35. **P. 43:** "I never knew…" Laura Ingalls Wilder: A Writer's Life, p. 33. **P. 43:** "One morning when…" Laura: The Life of Laura Ingalls Wilder, p. 144. **P. 44:** "The last thing…" Laura Ingalls Wilder: A Writer's Life, p. 36. **P. 46-47:** "great, new country…" Laura Ingalls Wilder: A Writer's Life, p. 40. **P. 48:** "There was one large…" Laura Ingalls Wilder: A Writer's Life, p. 41. **P. 49:** "sent out into the west…" Laura Ingalls Wilder: A Writer's Life, p. 42. **P. 50:** "Pa was standing…" Laura Ingalls Wilder: A Writer's Life, p. 45. **P. 50:** "Slowly at first…" Laura Ingalls Wilder: A Writer's Life, p. 43. **P. 51:** "The farm was home…" Laura: The Life of Laura Ingalls Wilder, p. 164. **P. 52:** "Snow drifts in one…" Laura: The Life of Laura Ingalls Wilder, p. 175. **P. 52:** "tall and quick…" Laura Ingalls Wilder's Little Town: Where History and Literature Meet, p. 62. **P. 54:** "Dad would walk…" I Remember Laura, p. 28. **P. 54:** "It seemed as though…" Laura Ingalls Wilder: A Writer's Life, p. 48. **P. 54-55:** "Hay does not hold…" I Remember Laura, p. 29. **P. 55:** "All the men in town…" Laura: The Life of Laura Ingalls Wilder, p. 175. **P. 56:** "I didn't much care…" Laura Ingalls Wilder: A Writer's Life, p. 53. **P. 57:** "to be perfectly truthful…" Laura Ingalls Wilder's Little Town: Where History and Literature Meet, p. 63. **P. 59-60:** "I was only…" Laura Ingalls Wilder: A Writer's Life, p. 56. **P. 60:** "I hadn't known…" Laura Ingalls Wilder: A Writer's Life, p. 63. **P. 61:** "he kissed me…" Laura: The Life of Laura Ingalls Wilder, p. 203. **P. 62:** "tree claim" Laura Ingalls Wilder: A Biography, p. 129. **P. 63:** "I learned to do…" Becoming Laura Ingalls Wilder: The Woman behind the Legend, p. 75. **P. 64-65:** "Nobody knew what would…" On the Way Home: The Diary of a Trip from South Dakota to Mansfield, Missouri, in 1894, p. 2. **P. 65:** "She is the best…" Laura: The Life of Laura Ingalls Wilder, p. 213. **P. 65:** "Laura's little baby…" Laura Ingalls Wilder: A Writer's

Life, p. 70. **P. 66:** "I quite well remember…" Laura Ingalls Wilder: A Writer's Life, p. 71. **P. 67:** "We went to live…" Becoming Laura Ingalls Wilder: The Woman behind the Legend, p. 87. **P. 68:** "we had no furniture…" Becoming Laura Ingalls Wilder: The Woman behind the Legend, p. 90. **P. 69:** "from six o'clock…" Laura Ingalls Wilder: A Writer's Life, p. 80. **P. 71:** "Worst crops we have seen…" On the Way Home: The Diary of a Trip from South Dakota to Mansfield, Missouri, in 1894, p. 15. **P. 71:** "Rose went out…" On the Way Home: The Diary of a Trip from South Dakota to Mansfield, Missouri, in 1894, p. 21. **P. 71:** "I went to a house…" On the Way Home: The Diary of a Trip from South Dakota to Mansfield, Missouri, in 1894, p. 17. **P. 72:** "It is a drowsy…" On the Way Home: The Diary of a Trip from South Dakota to Mansfield, Missouri, in 1894, p. 32. **P. 72:** "We breathe dust…" and "We stopped by…" On the Way Home: The Diary of a Trip from South Dakota to Mansfield, Missouri, in 1894, p. 50. **P. 72:** "And the very first…" On the Way Home: The Diary of a Trip from South Dakota to Mansfield, Missouri, in 1894, p. 62. **P. 72:** "Well, we are in…" On the Way Home: The Diary of a Trip from South Dakota to Mansfield, Missouri, in 1894, p. 65. **P. 73:** "There is everything…" On the Way Home: The Diary of a Trip from South Dakota to Mansfield, Missouri, in 1894, p. 74. **P. 73:** "never had talked so fast." A Little House Traveler: Writings from Laura Ingalls Wilder's Journeys Across America, p. 87. **P. 73:** "so much, much more…" On the Way Home: The Diary of a Trip from South Dakota to Mansfield, Missouri, in 1894, p. 77. **P. 75:** "would rather have…" and "The garden, my hens…" Laura: The Life of Laura Ingalls Wilder, p. 219. **P. 76:** "the horrid, snuffling…" The Ghost in the Little House: A Life of Rose Wilder Lane, p. 30. **P. 76-77:** "Winter evenings were…" A Little House Traveler: Writings from Laura Ingalls Wilder's Journeys Across America, p. 108. **P. 77:** "Because I loved…" The Ghost in the Little House: A Life of Rose Wilder Lane, p. 32. **P. 78:** "Our idea of an ideal…" Laura Ingalls Wilder: A Biography, p. 152. **P. 79:** "When I look around…" Laura: The Life of Laura Ingalls Wilder, p. 219-220. **P. 80:** "In a few years…" and "I was too shy…" Laura Ingalls Wilder: A Writer's Life, p. 90. **P. 81:** "landscapes of forest…" Laura: The Life of Laura Ingalls Wilder, p. 221. **P. 81:** "She hates kneading." Laura: The Life of Laura Ingalls Wilder, p. 221. **P. 81:** "Darkness overshadowed…" Laura Ingalls Wilder: A Writer's Life, p. 120. **P. 83:** "He drove me to…" The Ghost in the Little House: A Life of Rose Wilder Lane, p. 43. **P. 83:** "Rose Wilder…" The Ghost in the Little House: A Life of Rose Wilder Lane, p. 44. **P. 86:** "a purely wonderful car…" The Ghost in the Little House: A Life of Rose Wilder Lane, p. 57. **P. 87:** "friendly, interesting…" Laura Ingalls Wilder: A Writer's Life, p. 99. **P. 87:** "washing in buttermilk" and "It used to be…" Becoming Laura Ingalls Wilder: The Woman behind the Legend, p. 116. **P. 88:** "The effect is…" Laura Ingalls Wilder: A Writer's Life, p. 95. **P. 88:** "A.J. Wilder's…" Becoming Laura Ingalls Wilder: The Woman behind the Legend, p. 120. **P. 89:** "I simply can't…" A Little House Traveler: Writings from Laura Ingalls Wilder's Journeys Across America, pp. 129-130. **P. 90:** "I will be able…" A Little House Traveler: Writings from Laura Ingalls Wilder's Journeys Across America, p. 131. **P. 90:** "I wish you were…" A Little House Traveler: Writings from Laura Ingalls Wilder's Journeys Across America, p. 144. **P. 91:** "would probably pay…" A Little House Traveler: Writings from Laura Ingalls Wilder's Journeys Across America, pp. 131-132. **P. 92:** "At Land's End…" A Little House Traveler: Writings from Laura Ingalls Wilder's Journeys Across America, p. 152. **P. 92:** "We went nearer…" A Little House Traveler: Writings from Laura Ingalls Wilder's Journeys Across America, p. 155. **P. 92-93:** "Set on the hills…" A Little House Traveler: Writings from Laura Ingalls Wilder's Journeys Across America, p. 159. **P. 93:** "I do want…" A Little House Traveler: Writings from Laura Ingalls Wilder's Journeys Across America, p. 197. **P. 93:** "Rose and I are…" A Little House Traveler: Writings from Laura Ingalls Wilder's Journeys Across America, p. 212. **P. 95:** "We are in the midst…" I Remember Laura, p. 159. **P. 95-96:** "I knew of one…" I Remember Laura, p. 161. **P. 96:** "Not far from this…" I Remember Laura, p. 162. **P. 97:** "I have just…" The Ghost in the Little House: A Life of Rose Wilder Lane, p. 58. **P. 98:** "There is no reason…" Laura Ingalls Wilder: A Writer's Life, p. 105. **P. 99:** "I don't think…" Laura Ingalls Wilder: A Writer's Life, p. 118. **P. 99:** "Don't say those…" Laura Ingalls Wilder: A Writer's Life, p. 119. **P. 99:** "I feel simply…" The Ghost in the Little House: A Life of Rose Wilder Lane, p. 93. **P. 100:** "Like a dream…" The Ghost in the Little House: A Life of Rose Wilder Lane, p. 141. **P. 100:** "This life is…" The Ghost in the Little House: A Life of Rose Wilder Lane, p. 142. **P. 100:** "My mother is old…" The Ghost in the Little House: A Life of Rose Wilder Lane, p. 143. **P. 101:** "a darling cottage…" Laura Ingalls Wilder: A Writer's Life, p. 127. **P. 102:** "Don't be absurd…" Laura Ingalls Wilder: A Writer's Life, p. 116. **P. 103:** "At least your copy…" Laura Ingalls Wilder: A Writer's Life, p. 117. **P. 103:** "If the same material…" Laura Ingalls Wilder: A Writer's Life, p. 133. **P. 103-104:** "It didn't seem to…" Laura Ingalls Wilder: A Writer's Life, p. 7. **P. 104:** "I like the material…" I Remember Laura, p. 183. **P. 104:** "The book is not…" Laura Ingalls Wilder: A Writer's Life, p. 42. **P. 105:** "It does not belong…" Laura Ingalls Wilder: A Writer's Life, p. 29. **P. 105-106:** "Mother and daughter…" I Remember Laura, p. 145. **P. 106:** "It is a testimony…" I Remember Laura, p. 244. **P. 107:** "I somehow always…" The Ghost in the Little House: A Life of Rose Wilder Lane, p. 146. **P. 107:** "I have written you…" The Ghost in the Little House: A Life of Rose Wilder Lane, p. 264. **P. 109:** "Grace seems like…" A Little House Traveler: Writings from Laura Ingalls Wilder's Journeys Across America, p. 307. **P. 109:** "It all makes me…" A Little House Traveler: Writings from Laura Ingalls Wilder's Journeys Across America, p. 314. **P. 109:** "nearly in the place…" A Little House Traveler: Writings from Laura Ingalls Wilder's Journeys Across America, p. 311. **P. 110-111:** "My mother is now…" Laura Ingalls Wilder: A Writer's Life, p. 156. **P. 111:** "Mrs. Wilder has caught…" Becoming Laura Ingalls Wilder: The Woman behind the Legend, p. 208. **P. 111-112:** "I see the pictures…" Becoming Laura Ingalls Wilder: The Woman behind the Legend, p. 211. **P. 112:** "vowed she didn't…" Becoming Laura Ingalls Wilder: The Woman behind the Legend, p. 211. **P. 112-113:** "I wanted the children…" Laura Ingalls Wilder's Little Town: Where History and Literature Meet, p. 97. **P. 113:** "Without your help…" Little House, Long Shadow: Laura Ingalls Wilder's Impact on American Culture, p. 64. **P. 113:** "I would like to know…" Laura Ingalls Wilder: A Writer's Life, p. 157. **P. 113:** "Children who read it…" Laura: The Life of Laura Ingalls Wilder, p. 234. **P. 113:** "Oh, Mrs. Wilder did…" I Remember Laura, p. 112. **P. 113:** "Sometimes the mail…" I Remember Laura, p. 136. **P. 113-114:** "read in the bathtub…" Little House, Long Shadow: Laura Ingalls Wilder's Impact on American Culture, p. 128. **P. 114:** "We librarians are very…" Little House, Long Shadow: Laura Ingalls Wilder's Impact on American Culture, p. 124. **P. 114:** "I don't see how…" Laura Ingalls Wilder: A Writer's Life, p. 174. **P. 115:** "It has been rather trying…" Laura Ingalls Wilder: A Writer's Life, p. 48. **P. 116:** "I am very…" Becoming Laura Ingalls Wilder: The Woman behind the Legend, p. 251. **P. 117:** "There were always…" and "I don't know how…" I Remember Laura, p. 138. **P. 117:** "I owe Rose…" The Ghost in the Little House: A Life of Rose Wilder Lane, p. 334. **P. 118:** "While the pencil…" I Remember Laura, p. 268. **P. 119-120:** "Tumbled in a cardboard…" A Little House Traveler: Writings from Laura Ingalls Wilder's Journeys Across America, p. 123.

Index

Bibliography

Anderson, William. Laura Ingalls Wilder: A Biography. New York: HarperCollins, 1992. **Fellman, Anita Clair.** Little House, Long Shadow: Laura Ingalls Wilder's Impact on American Culture. Columbia, MO: University of Missouri Press, 2008. **Hill, Pamela Smith.** Laura Ingalls Wilder: A Writer's Life. South Dakota State Historical Society Press, 2007. **Hines, Stephen W.** Laura Ingalls Wilder: Little House in the Ozarks. New York: Galahad Books, 1996. **Hines, Stephen W.** "I Remember Laura" Nashville, TN: Thomas Nelson Publishers, 1994. **Holtz, William.** The Ghost in the Little House: A Life of Rose Wilder Lane. Columbia, MO: University of Missouri Press, 1993. **Lane, Rose Wilder. Ed., with introduction by Lauters, Amy Mattson.** The Rediscovered Writings of Rose Wilder Lane. Columbia, MO: University of Missouri Press, 2007. **Miller, John E.** Becoming Laura Ingalls Wilder: The Woman behind the Legend. Columbia, MO: University of Missouri Press, 1998. **Miller, John E.** Laura Ingalls Wilder's Little Town: Where History and Literature Meet. University Press of Kansas, 1994. **Romines, Ann.** Constructing the Little House: Gender, Culture, and Laura Ingalls Wilder. Amherst, MA: University of Massachusetts Press, 1997. **Wilder, Laura Ingalls.** On the Way Home: The Diary of a Trip from South Dakota to Mansfield, Missouri, in 1894. **Wilder, Laura Ingalls.** A Little House Traveler: Writings from Laura Ingalls Wilder's Journeys Across America. New York: HarperCollins, 2006. **Zochert, Donald.** Laura: The Life of Laura Ingalls Wilder. Chicago, IL: Henry Regnery Company, 1976.

Acknowledgments

Many thanks to Nicole Elzenga, Collections Manager of the Laura Ingalls Wilder Museum in Walnut Grove, Minnesota, for her expert review of this manuscript. And as always, I would like to thank my family for their continual love and support.

Picture Credits

FRONT COVER Photo by Laura Ingalls Wilder Home and Museum, Mansfield
BACK COVER Photo by Laura Ingalls Wilder Home and Museum, Mansfield
The photographs in this book are used with permission and through the courtesy of:
Herbert Hoover Presidential Library: pp. 6, 38, 57, 58B, 66, 73, 78, 79, 82, 83, 86 (2 insets), 90, 96, 98, 104, 109, 114, 119, 122TR. DK Images: p. 8. Keystone Area Historical Society: pp. 10, 122TL. Laura Ingalls Wilder Home and Museum, Mansfield: pp. 1, 2, 11, 22, 40, 54, 58T, 59, 60, 62, 65, 67, 74, 75, 76, 77, 80, 81, 84, 85, 86T, 87, 89, 94, 95, 98, 99, 100, 101, 102, 110, 112(all 3), 115, 116, 121, 122BC, 122B(all), 123TC,TR,BL,BR, 124-125(background), 126-127(background). Alamy Images:pp. 13, 122TC Danita Delimont; p. 61 Don Smetzer; p. 64 Nigel Cattlin. Corbis: pp. 14, 16, 19, 88, 108, 123TL Bettman; p. 18 Stapleton Collection; p. 44 Minnesota Historical Society; p. 71 James L. Amos. National Archives: pp. 15, 50. Library of Congress: pp. 5, 17, 30, 4, 122BL. Getty Images: pp. 20, 24, 32, 46, 53; p. 29 Roger Viollet; p. 120 Michael Ochs Archives. Minnesota Historical Society: pp. 25, 26, 31, 33, 48. Laura Ingalls Wilder Museum, Walnut Grove: pp. 34, 122BL. Laura Ingalls Wilder Memorial Society, De Smet:p. 35, 48B, 57B. Burr Oak Inn: p. 37. State Archives of the South Dakota Historical Society: pp. 51, 55, 68(all), 106. Iowa Braille and Sight Saving School: p. 56. Kansas State Historical Society: p. 70. San Francisco History Center, SF Public Library: pp. 90-91B, 92, 93, 106, p. 123BC.

BORDER IMAGES from left: Laura Ingalls Wilder Home and Museum, Mansfield(LIWHM); State Archives of the South Dakota Historical Society; DK Images; LIWHM; Library of Congress; LIWHM

About the Author

Tanya Lee Stone was an editor for 13 years before becoming a full-time writer. She is the author of nearly 90 books for young readers on topics that include science, nature, history, and biography. As a student at Oberlin College, she studied English, creative writing, history, and music. Later, she received a Masters in Education. Stone often travels to schools and conferences to talk about her books and writing for young people. To learn more, please visit www.tanyastone.com

Other DK Biographies you'll enjoy:

Marie Curie
Vicki Cobb
ISBN 978-0-7566-3831-3 paperback
ISBN 978-0-7566-3832-0 hardcover

Charles Darwin
David C. King
ISBN 978-0-7566-2554-2 paperback
ISBN 978-0-7566-2555-9 hardcover

Princess Diana
Joanne Mattern
ISBN 978-0-7566-1614-4 paperback
ISBN 978-0-7566-1613-7 hardcover

Amelia Earhart
Tanya Lee Stone
ISBN 978-0-7566-2552-8 paperback
ISBN 978-0-7566-2553-5 hardcover

Albert Einstein
Frieda Wishinsky
ISBN 978-0-7566-1247-4 paperback
ISBN 978-0-7566-1248-1 hardcover

Benjamin Franklin
Stephen Krensky
ISBN 978-0-7566-3528-2 paperback
ISBN 978-0-7566-3529-9 hardcover

Gandhi
Amy Pastan
ISBN 978-0-7566-2111-7 paperback
ISBN 978-0-7566-2112-4 hardcover

Harry Houdini
Vicki Cobb
ISBN 978-0-7566-1245-0 paperback
ISBN 978-0-7566-1246-7 hardcover

Helen Keller
Leslie Garrett
ISBN 978-0-7566-0339-7 paperback
ISBN 978-0-7566-0488-2 hardcover

Thomas Jefferson
Jacqueline Ching
ISBN 978-0-7566-4506-9 paperback
ISBN 978-0-7566-4506-9 hardcover

Joan of Arc
Kathleen Kudlinksi
ISBN 978-0-7566-3526-8 paperback
ISBN 978-0-7566-3527-5 hardcover

John F. Kennedy
Howard S. Kaplan
ISBN 978-0-7566-0340-3 paperback
ISBN 978-0-7566-0489-9 hardcover

Martin Luther King, Jr.
Amy Pastan
ISBN 978-0-7566-0342-7 paperback
ISBN 978-0-7566-0491-2 hardcover

Abraham Lincoln
Tanya Lee Stone
ISBN 978-0-7566-0834-7 paperback
ISBN 978-0-7566-0833-0 hardcover

Nelson Mandela
Lenny Hort & Laaren Brown
ISBN 978-0-7566-2109-4 paperback
ISBN 978-0-7566-2110-0 hardcover

Mother Teresa
Maya Gold
ISBN 978-0-7566-3880-1 paperback
ISBN 978-0-7566-3881-8 hardcover

Annie Oakley
Chuck Wills
ISBN 978-0-7566-2997-7 paperback
ISBN 978-0-7566-2986-1 hardcover

Pelé
Jim Buckley
ISBN 978-0-7566-2987-8 paperback
ISBN 978-0-7566-2996-0 hardcover

Eleanor Roosevelt
Kem Knapp Sawyer
ISBN 978-0-7566-1496-6 paperback
ISBN 978-0-7566-1495-9 hardcover

George Washington
Lenny Hort
ISBN 978-0-7566-0835-4 paperback
ISBN 978-0-7566-0832-3 hardcover

Look what the critics are saying about DK Biography!

"…highly readable, worthwhile overviews for young people…" —*Booklist*

"This new series from the inimitable DK Publishing brings together the usual brilliant photography with a historian's approach to biography subjects." —*Ingram Library Services*